GIANTS

GIANTS

WHAT I LEARNED ABOUT LIFE FROM
VINCE LOMBARDI AND TOM LANDRY

PAT SUMMERALL
and MICHAEL LEVIN

WILEY

John Wiley & Sons, Inc.

Published by John Wiley & Sons, Inc., Hoboken, New Jersey
Published simultaneously in Canada

Design by Forty-five Degree Design LLC

For general information about our other products and services, please contact our Customer Care Department within the United States at (800) 762-2974, outside the United States at (317) 572-3993 or fax (317) 572-4002.

Wiley also publishes its books in a variety of electronic formats. Some content that appears in print may not be available in electronic books. For more information about Wiley products, visit our web site at www.wiley.com.

Library of Congress Cataloging-in-Publication Data:

Summerall, Pat.
    Giants : what I learned about life from Vince Lombardi and Tom Landry / Pat Summerall and Michael Levin.
        p. cm.
    Includes index.
    ISBN 978-0-470-61159-3 (cloth); ISBN 978-0-470-90906-5 (ebk);
    ISBN 978-0-470-90907-2 (ebk); ISBN 978-0-470-90908-9 (ebk)
    1. Lombardi, Vince   2. Landry, Tom   3. Football coaches—United States—Biography.
4. New York Giants (Football team)   I. Levin, Michael.   II. Title.
    GV939.L6S85   2010
    796.332'64097471—dc22

                                                                        2010010786

Printed in the United States of America
10 9 8 7 6 5 4 3 2 1

Just as we were completing work on this book, my broadcasting partner and lifelong friend Tom Brookshier passed away. This book is dedicated to his memory, and to the memory of coaches Tom Landry and Vince Lombardi.

—P. S.

For my team: Suzanne, Chynna, Walter, Isaac, and Aliya.

—M. L.

CONTENTS

CONTENTS

ACKNOWLEDGMENTS

I'd like to thank my coauthor, Michael Levin, who was the first person to realize that a book about the lessons from my time with coaches Tom Landry and Vince Lombardi could be a success. I enjoyed our interviews, and I respect his knowledge of football.

Our time together also brought back many memories and made me realize the impact the two gentlemen, Landry and Lombardi, had on my entire life.

I'd also like to thank the members of Michael's team who worked so hard to make this book a reality: Nicole Rhoton, Carrie Pestruto, Teresa Spencer, and Mindy King.

Finally, Michael and I would both like to thank Sheryl Pidgeon, who made the connection between us and, therefore, made this book possible.

★ ★ ★ ★ ★ ★ ★ ★ ★ ★ ★ ★ ★

Introduction

During the 1958 New York Giants season, I had the honor of playing for two of the most elite coaches the game has ever known: Vince Lombardi and Tom Landry. Both would go on to become head coaches and lead dominating teams—the Green Bay Packers and the Dallas Cowboys, respectively—to glory. But in those days, they were starting out in the National Football League. They were serving as assistant coaches under Jim Lee Howell, then head coach of the Giants. Lombardi was the offensive coordinator, and Landry headed the team's defensive unit.

Playing the game back then—before teams had endless rosters and backups for almost every position—there was much less specialization than there is today. That meant I had the incredible luck of playing under both men, as a placekicker, a defensive end, and an offensive swing, filling in for different offensive positions when other players were hurt. I'm the only football player to have been coached by both Lombardi and Landry in the same season. It's an incredible convergence of circumstances that I'll never remember lightly. The example they set and the knowledge they exuded from their very cores had a profound effect on my playing, certainly. But more importantly, their guidance grew into not just a model for playing, but also a model for living that anyone would be proud to aspire to. They shaped me into the man I am.

In some ways, Landry and Lombardi were like night and day, but when it came to their values and their passion for the game, they were one man. For both of them, living well meant honoring three values: faith, family, and football. In that order. Landry was the one to claim that maxim—"faith, family, football"—out loud, but Lombardi lived it just as much. Each had his own way of showing it, though.

If you think back to the way they coached games, their sideline manners are perfect encapsulations of how they led their lives. Imagine watching a Cowboys game on TV back in the 1970s or 1980s, during the team's heyday. If the camera ever cut to a tight shot of Coach Landry standing on the sidelines, you'd have no idea whether his team was winning or losing. He wore the same stoic expression during both of his two Super Bowl title games, which the Cowboys won hands down. And his expression didn't change during that now famous 1981 NFC championship game against the San Francisco 49ers. As Dwight Clark caught that impossible pass from Joe Montana in the final minute, the pass that went down in history as "the Catch" and sealed the game for the 49ers, Landry watched, seemingly unmoved.

On the other hand, you could follow an entire Packers game, play by play, without once looking at the field if you just kept your eye trained on Coach Lombardi. The man was emotional, volatile, expressive. He paved the way for sideline manners like Bobby Knight's; he made rule by fear the status quo for pro coaching. But he didn't reserve his eruptions for the failed plays. If you did something well, if you made Lombardi proud, you knew it. I remember a Giants game once when I made a field goal that Lombardi had been against attempting. When I came off the field after scoring, he said to me, "You son of a bitch, you know you can't kick it that far," with nothing but warmth and affection. A lot of fans think of Lombardi's trademark grin as his defining feature, and so did we as players. We used to say he had the same number of teeth as anyone else, but his were all on top.

Both Lombardi and Landry had equal amounts of passion, but Lombardi let his overflow, while Landry kept his contained. Before I was traded to the Giants, I had never seen a level of devotion to excellence in football that could even rival Lombardi's or Landry's. It seems strange to admit, because I was already twenty-eight years old when I first signed with the Giants. I had been playing football without interruption for nearly fifteen years by then, since I was in high school. I had six professional seasons with the Lions and the Cardinals under my belt. And yet when I first arrived at training camp in the summer of 1958 and began learning under Lombardi and Landry, I had the distinct impression that I had never truly played the game before.

CHAPTER 1

The Cardinals: Not the Way Football Is Supposed to Be

I vividly remember my introduction to the National Football League. I had played football at the University of Arkansas from 1949 to 1951, doing well enough to participate in the college all-star game, and in my last year of school, the Detroit Lions picked me in the fourth round of the NFL draft. Before this opportunity arose, I had done some thinking about a career coaching high school ball and teaching history or whatever they assigned me to teach. But I also knew in the back of my mind that I wasn't tired of playing football yet and wanted to continue to play if I could. So I took the Lions' offer . . . only to be injured early in the 1952 season. I was benched, and by the next year, they had traded me.

When I signed with the Chicago Cardinals in 1953, I was aware that they had played in NFL championship games in 1947 and 1948, winning the championship in 1947, so I figured they were pretty good. You have to realize that back then pro football was not "America's game" by any means; it was basically an afterthought and didn't get much media or television coverage, and even when it did, not everyone in America had a television of their own to watch it on. The sports of the day were college football, baseball, horse racing, and boxing. So even though I was an avid football player and fan, I didn't know every statistic about NFL teams the way people do nowadays.

I went into my pro career with a naive idea of what it would be like to play in the NFL, but by the end of my first day, the unvarnished reality of pro ball had wiped out my silly fantasies as completely as the first sustained nuclear chain reaction, under the stands in the stadium where we practiced, had changed the world. But I'm getting ahead of myself.

The Cardinals' training camp was held in the facilities at the University of Chicago, and they put us up in the nearby Piccadilly Hotel. The second I walked through the hotel doors, I understood that a couple of championship games and a championship hadn't exactly secured the Cardinals' fortunes. The Piccadilly was on the gritty South Side of Chicago, and it had once been grand, housing a three-thousand-seat theater in the 1920s. But when people lost interest in vaudeville, they lost interest in the hotel, too, and now the place definitely qualified as a dump. The lobby was a musty, red velvet monument to another era. The elevator was the old-fashioned kind that you had to get in and operate yourself. This was nothing like the luxury NFL players take for granted today.

When I showed up at the University of Chicago for practice, I went straight to the locker room. The first person I saw when I walked in the door was Plato Andros, an All-American from Oklahoma, sitting in the hot tub, casually smoking a cigar, and reading the *Daily Racing Form*. The locker room was just as dirty and despondent as the hotel. Some of the lockers stood ajar, their metal doors too bent to fit their frames. The floor was sticky with something I was glad I couldn't identify, and I was sure it hadn't felt the touch of a mop in months. I thought, "This is not the way football is supposed to be."

Plato took his cigar out of his mouth and sneered at the look on my face. "Big leagues my ass," he said with a laugh.

No kidding.

Out on the field, I looked up at the stands during a break in practice and noticed that they were covered in what seemed to be tarpaper and had little smokestacks coming up out of the bleachers. I turned to fullback Johnny Olszewski, who was a good player and one of the friendlier guys.

"What the heck is that? Why are those little smokestacks sticking out of the bleachers?"

He gave me a look and told me that the atomic bomb had been developed in the stadium. During World War II, the University of Chicago football team had been disbanded so that chemists and other scientists could work here on the production of a controlled and self-maintaining nuclear chain reaction using uranium. I was too shocked to reply or to do anything but reel from the knowledge that a lethal nuclear weapon had been developed right where we were tossing a pigskin around as casually as kids.

After practice was finished, we went to Comiskey Park, the regular-season home stadium of the Cardinals, for a meeting. And there, yet again, I met with a stark reality. At Arkansas and Detroit, we may not have been pampered, but at least everything we had was clean and acceptable. Here the chairs were bent and uncomfortable and the locker room was dirty. The equipment and uniforms were ill-fitting and made with poor-quality materials, and I had to share a locker (if you could call it a locker) with another teammate. I guess I didn't get a private locker because I joined the team late, but even if they *had* given me my own, I doubt that it would have been much of an improvement. The locker I shared was just a stall with two nails: he had a nail and I had a nail, and that's where we hung our gear.

We did not have any offices or private rooms, like players have in modern football stadiums, either. The training room and taping facility were all part of the locker room. Players, trainers, the equipment manager, and the coaches all dressed and went about their respective businesses together—there were no offices for coaches or rooms for the trainers or equipment manager.

And since there were no media following the teams, there was no need to have a room where the players could get away from the journalists, as is necessary today. There also was no separate cafeteria for lunch. Basically, the defensive unit would go in one corner of the locker room and the offensive unit would go in another, and if you wanted lunch, you brought a brown bag.

But even though there were offensive and defensive meetings, there were no meetings after practice or special-team meetings. If you were on the kickoff team, as I was, you just were on the kickoff team. No one talked to you about staying in your lane or what portion of the field you were to cover. The coaches for the defensive and offensive units ran their meetings, and that was it.

Our head coach was Big Joe Stydahar, who had led the Los Angeles Rams to NFL championship games, winning in 1951, and then was hired by the Cardinals. He was the only man I ever knew who could chew tobacco and drink whiskey at the same time, and I think he often did both while he was coaching. He didn't have much of a staff: maybe four or five people, none of whom had the teaching ability I was later exposed to when I went to the Giants. They pretty much had you line up and play your positions. There was very little teaching or work on technique.

The plays were very minimal—like our facilities, they left something to be desired. Of course, plays don't have to be complicated to be good, but I started to feel suspicious when I realized we had only a few plays that looked like they even had a chance of being successful. I was a three-way player: I was a kicker, a defensive end, and an alternate on offense, and I got to know the "defensive strategy" like the back of my hand. And that, truth be told, didn't take much effort. We stayed in the same defense all the time; there was no zone, no man-to-man, nothing like that. You had a man to cover, and you stayed with him, plain and simple.

Unfortunately for my teammates, the general lack of motivation on the Cardinals was catching. The players ended up reflecting back the same disinterest that the management showed them. They were a depressed, unhappy bunch of guys. Any potential they had was sapped by the atmosphere of the place, and I couldn't see in them any remnants of the 1947 and 1948 championship team I had remembered. The only player left from that time was Charley Trippi, an All-American and an outstanding rookie in 1947. I had seen him play in college in the Georgia-Florida game and knew what a reputation he had. I also knew the college reputations of some others on the team, but none of those reputations seemed to have any staying power in Chicago. Trippi had already seen his best days by the time I got there. Yet he was still the foundation the Cardinals rallied around. The other players were good people and good friends, but they either didn't have the skills or didn't have the motivation to rise above our environment and to succeed even without teaching.

I realized right away that the atmosphere was not conducive to being a championship-quality team. It was an existence more than a profession. I was paid $5,500 and, as I said, I was both a kicker and a regular on defense, as well as an alternate on offense, so they got their money's worth out of me. At the time, though, I thought the pay was pretty good. I remember I got up to $7,500 during my fourth year and thought I was in the chips.

When I joined the team, the kicker the Cardinals had was drunk most of the time, which was probably why they were scouting me. His attitude was the attitude of most of the players. They all had the outlook of "We're not going to win many games anyway, so why should we try?" Well, we didn't win many games, that was for sure. Our '53 season was 1–10–1. What's more, the fans were never that supportive, though that was typical of most NFL fans at the time. On a good day, we had ten or eleven thousand—twenty thousand or more if we were playing the Bears—at Comiskey Park, which easily could have seated fifty-five thousand. It was almost like the audience was attending a private scrimmage; when the fans booed you, you could hear what they were saying, and it could get pretty personal. Some of the players even got into arguments with the people in the stands.

Our single win was against the Bears at the end of the year. Before the game, our coach took all of our checks, wrapped them in a rubber band, threw them in the middle of the locker room, and said, "Fight for 'em, you assholes."

He told us that if we didn't beat the Bears, none of us would get paid. He also gave us each a little commentary on our performance in the previous game. "You have no ability." "You're gutless." "Why are you in the NFL?" I suppose this was his last-ditch effort to motivate us. I do know that it certainly struck fear into our hearts.

Back then, there were only twelve teams in the league, and the player limit for each team was thirty-three men. If you were on a team that had trouble making ends meet, like the Cardinals, players were cut so there were fewer people to pay. If there were two players of equal talent, but one was getting a higher salary, you can bet that the higher-paid player would be released. Economics dictated cutting as many players as possible, so each of us really had to play our position and earn our keep. Finishing the season with twenty-five players was considered being in good shape. A team would have two quarterbacks, backup linemen on both sides of the ball, a backup defensive back, and a backup running back in addition to the eleven who started, and that just about made up the whole team. Today some teams have twenty assistant coaches. That's how radically the game has changed.

If somebody got hurt, he often had to play through it, unless the injury was grave. In one instance, our offensive tackle Len Teeuws hurt his ankle at Comiskey Park. He was lying on the ground in agony. The trainer came out; actually he was not a trainer, but a podiatrist by trade. Len had been abusive to the trainer in the locker room, so before he would shoot Len with painkiller, the trainer said, "Are you going to give me any more shit in the locker room?"

Len promised that he wouldn't cause any more trouble and then the trainer threw some alcohol on his pants and shot him right through his uniform. The poor guy had to get up after that and keep playing. We had no backup to cover him. Today an injury like that would have taken him off his foot for three or four weeks.

Getting injured was the biggest fear. The second was that our positions would be taken away; in fact, it was something we discussed every day. Players would break down the team as a pastime, talking about who they thought would be cut next. There was very little sense of camaraderie among the Cardinals. Instead, there were cliques of guys who stayed close together. Fear brought people together, and you were careful not to make good friends with someone you knew was on the borderline. We all knew Charley Trippi was going to stay, but there was not much job security for the rest of us. The rest of the team had the mentality of "Maybe, today, it's going to be you."

I certainly didn't think when I first walked into that hotel on the South Side that I would be spending the next five years of my life with the Cardinals; there was no guarantee I would even be there from week to week. And being a kicker certainly didn't make me feel like an essential part of the team. It didn't occur to people at that time that kicking was an important part of the game. I know that today, the Dallas Cowboys send their kickers from their practice field to Cowboys Stadium daily, so they can get used to the wind currents, the target they pick out in the stands, and so on. But back then, I only practiced kicking maybe three or four times a week—and even then, it was by my own volition.

I never could get anyone to hold for me, much less snap the ball from center, so I never got to practice much. The coaches didn't assign me any help—they just told me I was the kicker. While I was practicing, I had to build myself a little dirt tee, kick the ball from it, and then run and get the ball myself—just like a little kid playing on a sandlot. Because I was playing full-time defense as well as kicking, I was often too tired to practice on my own. In those days, practically the only time I practiced kicking off was during a game.

The guys in the game who were going to return kickoffs were the backup running back, backup quarterback, and backup defensive back. They'd practice with me until they were satisfied with their own game, but if I wanted to kick fifty times, it was too much for them. I would have perhaps ten warm-up kicks from increasing distances of ten yards, maybe on one side of the field, maybe not. It's amazing that I was any good at all, especially when you consider the resources available to a kicker nowadays. All of today's kickers are soccer-style kickers, first off, and they can practice and keep practicing. Kicking off the instep of your foot doesn't take as much out of you as kicking the ball head-on, so kicking isn't as wearing on them. In addition, there are men assigned to hold the ball, catch the ball, shag it, and throw it back to the center. There's somebody whose only role is to snap the ball—there's a deep snapper on every team who usually is a backup quarterback. That kind of help for kickers simply didn't exist on most teams when I was playing in the mid-1950s.

In fact, kicking was pretty much an afterthought, much in the way pro football was basically an afterthought in American sports. Lou "the Toe" Groza, the first well-known kicker, made people start to realize the importance of kickers and how they could turn a game around. Groza kicked the winning sixteen-yard field goal in the final seconds of the 1950 NFL championship game for the Cleveland Browns against the Rams. However, the Browns' electrifying win had virtually no effect on the league.

The circumstances of the win were not highly publicized in newspapers or the radio. The game was televised, but that didn't mean so much in those days. Television was not as ubiquitous as it is now, and even if you had a set, you probably were watching something else. In fact, the first game I remember seeing on television was the Rams versus the Browns the year *after* Groza's win.

NFL coaches were probably conscious of how the game was won, but just barely. They kept the mind-set of having the kicker work on his own and did not consider kicking to be an integral part of the game, but eventually kicking did work its way into coaching strategy. Paul Brown, the head coach for the Browns, appreciated the importance of three points and how the complexion of a game could change with the success of the kicker. He even assigned a defensive back to hold for Groza. Of course, it was a little bit easier to make a field goal then than it is today, since the goal post sat directly on the goal line, but three points were still three points.

Although on that first day at the Piccadilly Hotel I wasn't sure about my future or if I had made the right choice, after the end of the '53 season I don't remember wanting to quit. During training, I had determined that I would do my best—after all, playing football wasn't out of my system—and once I made friends with some of my teammates, the sense of fellowship I felt with them and our "us against the world" stance was enough for me to be anxious to return for the next season. There was no such thing as free agency back then, so besides some new member we might gain from the draft, I knew the team would basically remain the same.

During the off-season I went back home to backwoods Lake City, Florida, where I definitely wasn't hailed as a sports star. People would ask me, "What have you been doing?" and "Where have you been?" The Cardinals' games were broadcast in Chicago, but that was about it, and as a result, not many people in Florida knew that I was a pro football player. When they found out, they'd often ask when I was going to get a *real* job—they didn't see playing pro football as a career of any consequence. If I had told them I was playing professional baseball, on the other hand, I probably would have been welcomed like a returning war hero.

Ironically, most of the stadiums we played in were made for baseball, not football, which just shows how unpopular the sport was. Wrigley Field in Chicago, Forbes Field in Pittsburgh, Shibe Park in Philadelphia, Cleveland Stadium, the Polo Grounds in New York, Briggs Stadium in Detroit, Griffith Stadium in Washington, and of course, Comiskey Park were all baseball stadiums where NFL teams competed. There were only a handful of football-only stadiums in the entire NFL. Kezar Stadium, home of the San Francisco 49ers; Los Angeles Memorial Coliseum, where the Rams played; and the Green Bay Packers' City Stadium were the only strictly football stadiums. What with playing in arenas often far too big or far too small, little money, no television, and not much interest, it is a miracle that the NFL was able to survive the 1950s. The Cardinals were especially lucky to survive the 1950s, too.

Our 1954 season was only slightly better than our previous season had been. We beat Pittsburgh and Washington, giving us a 2–10 record. In 1955, there was a head-coaching change: Ray Richards replaced Big Joe Stydahar. Richards was a real gentleman and very low-key, although he was in no way inspirational. He had a good knowledge of the game. He had played in the NFL, was Stydahar's assistant coach with the Los Angeles Rams, and was a coach for a while with the Baltimore Colts. He was not much of a coach, though. We finished the 1955 season with a 4–7–1 record, outclassed in talent, coaching, organization, and every facet of the game by teams such as the Browns. Nevertheless,

I remember beating the Browns, 9–7, in the first game of the 1956 season. I kicked three field goals in the game, and as I was walking back to the sidelines, Paul Brown, their legendary coach, walked next to me. Amid what seemed like the first Cardinals fans' hollering and cheering I'd ever heard, he said, "Enjoy it now, son, because it's never going to happen again." Ironically, though, we beat the Browns again at the end of the year by an even bigger margin, 24–7, giving us a 7–5 record and putting us just out of the playoffs. Even then, the wins still didn't bring out the crowds.

We finished with the second-best record in the East, and I mainly credit our success not to Coach Richards, but rather to our running back Eli Mattson. Like a lot of excellent football recruits at that time, he had just returned from the service. The other factor that contributed to our wins was the split T, a play that was in vogue in college ball. We had a quarterback named Lamar McHan, who I played with at Arkansas, who could run the split T. It was rarely used in pro football, so they weren't prepared to stop it.

In the split T, the quarterback was the option runner—he either kept the ball or pitched it out. The splits in the offensive line were wider than they had ever been in pro football. The guard was two yards away from the center, the tackle was two yards from the guard, and every team had two tight ends who were split out even farther. This spread the field out quite a bit and involved more running than the conventional T formation.

The quarterback took the ball from the center, started down the line of scrimmage, and then pitched it back to one of the running backs or kept it himself. Ideally, he would run himself and not have to pitch the ball out. The disadvantage of the play was that the quarterback did a lot of running and, accordingly, his likelihood of being injured drastically increased, which is why more of the pro teams didn't adopt the play sooner. We'd start our games with the split T, which confused the opposing team and gave us a good head start.

Although it seemed that our losing streak was fading away, things never turned around financially for the Cardinals' ownership. The quality of the facility and our uniforms were the same, and over the course of those years, we still lived with the fear that each week would be our last. When the Players' Association was formed, I was one of the first people to join. Our captain, Jack Jennings, who was an offensive tackle, was instrumental in starting it. He was very active in the beginning of the association, as was Abe Gibron, a guard with the Browns, who later went to the Bears and then became a head coach at Tampa Bay. As a matter of fact, Paul Brown released Abe because of his Players' Association activity.

The Packers and the Browns first formed the NFL Players' Association in 1956. It was very shaky in the beginning and they were very careful not to call it a union. Being a charter member, as I was, wasn't a thing you wanted to publicize. If ownership knew, your chances of being released went up. I used to talk about the association with Jennings, about what players ought to be guaranteed in compensation and such things. Back then, you had to pay for your own shoes and for meals on Sundays, since the cafeteria at training camp didn't give dinners that night. At its conception, that's what the Players' Association was all about: dinner on Sunday nights and shoes, not health insurance or pensions.

It's amazing to think how much times have changed since then. There we were, sneaking around, trying to find a way to gently ask for a single pair of shoes, when today players practically have to fend off sportswear companies desperate to hand them free merchandise. When I was broadcasting a Dallas Cowboys game once, I looked in Emmett Smith's locker and was amazed at what I saw. He had a contractual deal with some sporting line, and there must have been 150 pairs of shoes in his locker—box after box of shoes that had never been worn. He could have practically shod the entire Eastern Conference in my time.

Not every player joined the Players' Association, obviously. I think that ownership knew what was going on, but I never got in trouble for my membership like Gibron did, though I did end up leaving the Cardinals. The truth was, even though I was making some progress with the Players' Association, I had begun toying with the idea of retiring. I'd had enough of the depressing situation with the Cardinals. I didn't have my future without football really mapped out, but teaching or coaching seemed like possibilities. And my wife, Kathy, fully supported the idea of my retiring. Life as a football wife was difficult, especially with the Cardinals, and she did not like it. About ten or twelve other players were married, and our wives always worried for us. Because we had no job security and anyone could be ousted at any time, there was a sense of attrition, as if we were in a war instead of the NFL. And since there was no security for us, there was no security for our wives.

I met Kathy in high school but didn't really get to know her until she finished college. She was four years younger than I, and when we were in high school that was a big age difference, but when I came back from college and when I visited in the off-season after beginning my career in the pros, the difference became smaller. Unlike most of the college girls I'd gone out with, she was a grounded girl, soft-spoken and religious. I saw her on occasion when a bunch of us would go water-skiing or fishing. I remember on one of those outings, my cousin Mike pointed to her and said, "That's who you ought to go out with, that gal there."

After we had been dating for a while, I asked her to marry me. I was twenty-five years old, all of my friends were married, and it seemed like the thing to do. Everyone called us an *almost* perfect couple, "almost" because we hadn't exchanged vows yet.

We enjoyed just dating and being a couple, though. We even spent a summer working at a camp together. She was a counselor and I was a lifeguard, and working together made us closer than ever.

Once I had proposed, I had to talk to her father, who was a gruff, tough military man. He asked me if I had any money, and I said I had some war bonds and a little money set aside from football. I told him that I planned to go back to training camp and get married after the 1956 season was over. He took charge, however, and said, "No. If you're going to do it, let's get on with it," so we were married before training camp.

Kathy came with me to Chicago. She didn't have a warm coat at the time, and I remember her almost freezing to death. All of us lived in the Piccadilly Hotel, and one time when I came back from practice, I couldn't find her. She was buried down in the bed, next to the radiator, trying to stay warm. When I found her that way, I knew we had to make some major adjustments. She didn't like things in Chicago at all—it was a pretty sad situation, actually. Some of the wives would get together to play bridge or go shopping. They would all go to the games together and sit by themselves in a section. And they didn't even get good seats, which was surprising when you considered how few tickets the Cardinals sold.

Of course, there weren't that many fans anyway. There was never any sort of instance where we were noticed on the streets of Chicago, unless it was for being bigger than everybody else. Even the people at the hotel, who knew we were football players, didn't give us any breaks or preferential treatment because of it. The Bears, on the other hand, were the darlings and elite of Chicago; we were the stepchildren. They got all the publicity in the papers, and their games were sold out every weekend. We were lucky if we got any mention by the media, which is why we only had those ten or twelve thousand antagonistic fans in our stadium.

What really tipped the balance for me was that Comiskey Park was in a dangerous part of town. It wasn't a place where you wanted to bring your cars or your kids. While we players were never worried for our own safety, we were definitely concerned for our wives when they came down. It wasn't easy to be married under those circumstances. There was no job security, and we had to live in two different places: Chicago during the football season and, for me and Kathy, Lake City in the off-season.

By the end of the '57 season, I'd started to wonder if my football days were over. But then, surprisingly, the Cardinals got a new head coach, a man named Pop Ivy. He came from the Canadian Football League and was supposed to have all these new philosophies about how to play the game, though I knew very little about him at the time. When the Cardinals hired Pop Ivy, he said that things were going to be different. He was going to open up the offense and run what they had run in Canada—some sort of double wing play that hadn't been seen in the NFL. I wasn't sure where I fit into that plan, so I called him and had a long conversation in which he told me that he had great plans for me as a key player and that I should consider playing some more. He assured me that I was a cornerstone, a building block, and a vital part of the team. I felt good about that, and it occurred to me that my future might be more secure than I thought—maybe even the playoffs were ahead of me. I shelved any thoughts of retirement and began to look forward to a new season and a new beginning with the Cardinals.

Of course, I never got that new beginning with Chicago. Two weeks after I received all those assurances from Ivy about my importance to the team, I was standing in the post office in Lake City, Florida, glancing at the sports pages of the local newspaper. That's when I read that I had been traded . . . to the New York Giants.

CHAPTER 2

The Bigger the Dream, the Bigger the Backup Plan

I was lucky that I was even able to be part of the NFL, let alone the Giants. I was born with a clubfoot and my entire right leg essentially twisted backward. At that time this was the kind of congenital condition that was considered inoperable. Most doctors assumed I'd use a wheelchair, or at best walk in braces, for the rest of my life. But thanks to the pioneering work of a general practitioner in Lake City named Dr. Harry Bates, who offered to treat my leg with an experimental procedure, I proved the prevailing thinking wrong. Dr. Bates fixed my leg by breaking it, turning it around, and resetting it. I underwent the surgery when I was an infant, and we knew immediately that it had been successful—in that I'd be able to walk normally. But Dr. Bates still cautioned us that I'd probably never be able to run, and certainly not play sports with the other boys.

My parents divorced before I was born, and because of my mother's difficult second marriage, I was mostly raised by my paternal grandmother. I never actually knew her age, but she was already becoming frail when I was a boy. Nevertheless, she encouraged my love of sports enthusiastically, so much so that she'd drag a chair out to the front yard so she could sit and catch my tosses. I'd gently throw the ball to her, then jog over to pick it up, jog a few yards out again, and toss—over and over. She didn't have a lot of range of motion sitting in that chair, so I had to learn to be pretty accurate tossing a football.

Of course, my grandmother couldn't throw, so when I wanted to practice catching, I would play with my cousin Mike or toss a ball up on the roof or against the house and let it bounce back. I would do that for hours, letting the ball bang and bang against the house, but my grandmother never once complained.

As I grew older, Dr. Bates's warning that I might never be able to run seemed to fade into the background. I would see other boys running, jumping, and playing, and I'd give it a try and find that I could do everything the others could. Over time it started to feel like I'd never had a bad leg. The idea that I'd never be able to play sports was nothing more than a distant nightmare, hazy in my memory.

When I entered the local high school, Columbia High, I had my mind set on playing every sport. I joined the football team, basketball team, and even played tennis. Back then, tennis wasn't exactly the game of choice for rural southern kids, so I didn't have a lot of competition in northern Florida. My grandmother lived right near Young's Park, where there were two tennis courts, and I got to be good enough that I was entered as my school's sole participant in the conference tournament in my junior year. I was matched against guys who had played for much longer than I had, but I still won the title. After the tournament was finished, I wanted to compete at the state level, but there was no school bus to take me to the tournament, in Fort Lauderdale. My grandmother didn't drive, either, so in the end, I packed my stuff and hitchhiked the whole 317 miles.

Everyone from Lake City thought I was nuts for going and that I wouldn't stand a chance against the serious tennis players from southern Florida. I didn't end up winning the tournament, but I got the runner-up trophy. I carried it all the way back home, raising it aloft to flag down drivers for a ride.

Playing tennis really helped with my agility, which I think was one of the reasons I made the all-conference football team.

Basketball was my favorite sport, though. That year, my school went to the state tournament in basketball as well as football. We fought our way there, playing close games against some of our biggest adversaries in the Northeast Conference, including Live Oak, another small town, just twenty-six miles away. We played them in every sport and had a great rivalry. We even had a traveling trophy with them. It was just an old oak bucket, but we sure went crazy trying to hang on to it as long as we could.

Columbia High didn't win any state titles my senior year, but I did make the all-conference and all-state teams in football and basketball. We also started our first baseball team that year, and I played first base. I was the town's star athlete, so there were high expectations about my college career. Just about everyone kept telling me to go to the University of Florida and be a Gator—including the coaches at the University of Florida, who started recruiting me relentlessly. But I was determined to be a multisport athlete, and the Gator football coaches were clear that I'd have to let basketball go. So I started searching for a school that would let me play both sports, which was how I found the University of Arkansas. They gave me a football scholarship and said I could play basketball, too.

The Arkansas coaches informed us that if we weren't scholars, the education curriculum was a good choice if we wanted to keep up grades eligible for the team, so I declared myself an education major. I had promised myself, my family, and Coach Hobart Hooser, the football line coach, that I'd study hard and attend classes, but after practicing and playing two sports—not to mention enjoying the social life of a college athlete—my goal grades slipped from "good" to "good enough." I was working my ass off in football, though. I was playing both offense and defense, and by the time my sophomore year rolled around, I became the team's primary kickoff and field goal man. I was spending more time on the bench in basketball than I cared for, so I quit basketball and focused on football.

Even though I had to give up basketball, my reason for being at Arkansas in the first place, I still thoroughly enjoyed my time there. But suddenly, in the midst of living the college life, I got a call from my father that seemed to freeze everything in place. My grandmother had died. Her health had been declining for a long time, but my father told me she went peacefully. He went on to say that I shouldn't try to come to the funeral, because it was a long trip and I would have to miss classes and practices. I think what he was really concerned about was that he didn't have the extra money to pay my way home, though he didn't say that. I thought about going anyway. It bothered me not to be there for her when she had been there for me, always. She had cheered me on and been my advocate—even when my own father and mother didn't bother to come to my games. To this day, I still wish I'd found a way to go to her funeral.

Even though I hadn't played baseball since my senior year in high school, I got a tryout with the St. Louis Cardinals organization the summer before my junior year. They said that they were always looking for good athletes and signed me onto their Class C minor league team in Lawton, Oklahoma. I didn't have to worry about wrecking my college eligibility because they didn't pay us to play. On that team, I played alongside Mickey Mantle's twin brothers, Roy and Ray, and we had a few games against their future legend of a brother in the Western Association. Mantle was a powerful switch hitter even then. He had incredible speed, and although he would make fielding errors, you could tell he was destined to be a baseball star.

I, however, clearly had no such destiny in baseball. After that season, my baseball career was over. My minor league coach said to me, "If you've still got a chance to play college football next season, you better take it."

I took his hint and after my senior year at Arkansas, I was the Detroit Lions' fourth-round pick in the 1952 draft. Detroit general manager Russ Thomas, a former Lions player himself, came to Fayetteville to sign me. Before he came down, he implied that I'd already made the team and was ensured a substantial contract. After I heard that, there were several nights of hard partying with my friends at our favorite bar, Hog's Heaven, and I put round after round on my tab. Thomas found me at Hog's Heaven when he came down to sign me and told me that all Lions players took the same $5,000 per year salary for the sake of team unity, saying, "There are no stars and no jealousy."

That didn't sound right to me and I said that I'd heard that some of my teammates who had been drafted were getting signing bonuses.

"We don't give signing bonuses," he replied. He told me that if they gave me a bonus or raised my salary, they would have to raise the salaries of everyone on the team.

All the same, I couldn't believe that big-name Lions such as Doak Walker, Bobby Layne, and Leon Hart would have the same salary as a rookie who hadn't played a down yet. Things didn't seem to add up to me, and I let Thomas know it. After a lot of back and forth, he backed down and agreed to increase his offer to $6,000 a year with a $500 signing bonus. When he finally caved, I remember thinking, "At least it'll pay off my bar tab."

When I got to training camp in Ypsilanti, I found out Thomas had indeed been pulling my leg. Veteran players such as Layne, who was the team captain, earned a lot more than the rest of us. During the season, most of the guys lived in cheap suburban hotels. Some players were barely scraping by, especially those with families. Even the team's top draft pick that year, University of Texas guard Harley Sewell, didn't have enough money for a decent suit. But Layne, who had also gone to the University of Texas, took care of him and hired a tailor to measure Sewell for a couple of new suits so Sewell could uphold the Longhorn image. Back then, players' salaries were not subject to media scrutiny, and most players didn't have agents pushing for top dollar. We weren't even paid for preseason exhibition games.

It was during an exhibition game that everything seemed to finally click for me, and I had a great day on both offense and defense. We were going over the game film after practice a few days later and the coach praised a block I made on the punt return. The film was so grainy that he couldn't tell who it was, but he pointed and said, "That's a hell of a block."

Only a few days later, just as I was starting to feel at home with the Lions, I pulled a hamstring running a simple pass pattern. I still hadn't officially made the team yet and was worried that my injury might mess things up for me. Back then, the Lions had their players wear matching dress suits on road trips, as most pro teams did. I knew that I'd made the team despite my injury when Larry Gersh, the team tailor, came over to my locker to make an appointment for a fitting. The equipment manager also informed me that he had ordered me a pair of square-toed kicking shoes, which further assuaged my fears. It was a bit of an anticlimax, but it was definitely better to get a team suit and kicking shoes than a plane ticket back home.

It was a short-lived victory, though. During our second game of the season, against the Rams, I got a compound fracture when I was cut-blocked while trying to block fullback Paul "Tank" Younger. Back in Detroit, I slipped and fell down some stairs, compounding the compound fracture. I had to have another operation and the doctors placed pins inside each bone with little hooks sticking out, so the pins could be removed. Then they put my arm in a big cast and me on the sidelines for the rest of the season.

My injury made me realize that I couldn't depend on an NFL paycheck for the rest of my life, so in the off-season, I reenrolled at Arkansas for spring semester graduate classes and got a graduate degree in history. After I was traded to the Chicago Cardinals, I worked as a teacher in the off-season and as a produce farmer with my friend P. A. Browning, the principal at the junior high school where I was teaching. We planted watermelons, bell peppers, tomatoes, and squash. It was more work than I'd ever done in my life, but in our first year, we had perfect growing conditions and a prime market. We each ended up with $50,000 in profits, which was nearly ten times what I made as a pro football player. I actually stayed with it for about five years, and I gained a new appreciation for football after a couple seasons of rough farm work, along with a new physique. Catching, carrying, and packing watermelons had made my hands and arms much stronger, and I went back to the Cardinals' training camp in 1954 in the best shape of my life.

The Cardinals, as I've said, didn't quite live up to my expectations. After a few years, the glory of football started to wear off, and so did the novelty of farming. We had one very good growing year and then a couple of not-so-good years. By the time I started the 1957 season with the Cardinals, my plans for the future were looking a little shaky on both the football and the farming fronts. We ended the season with a discouraging 3–9 record, and I started seriously contemplating quitting pro football. That's when Pop Ivy came on board and said to me, "Pat, you're one of our building blocks, one of the keys to our success. You're going to play both ways and be our kicker. We're counting on you." I never found out what made him stop counting.

CHAPTER 3

"React Like a Football Player"

When I stepped into the room for the first Giants team meeting of the 1958 season in Salem, Oregon, I could already tell I was in a different league. There were legendary players there, from Roosevelt Brown to Frank Gifford, the likes of whom I'd never expected to see on a single roster, let alone expected to play with.

The room was alive. Those who had played together before were absorbed in catching up after the off-season, and those of us who were new were still trying to take it all in. I remember that in the middle of all that excitement and noise and electricity, an assistant coach arrived to call roll. But he didn't stand a chance in that atmosphere. He'd call out a name, only to have it drowned by the laughter and conversation. He was standing at the front of the room, flustered and frustrated, unable to get through his list.

Then, all of a sudden, a man stepped into the room, and a hush fell over the team. He was short, almost stout, and he had on a pair of thick horn-rimmed glasses. If I had passed him on the street, I wouldn't have glanced twice at him. Little did I know that that season, he would become one of the two most influential coaches of my career, and that he would go on to earn the reputation of one of football's best, a champion and an idol. At the time, he looked like just another office manager.

He cleared his throat once, and the room went completely silent.

I was sitting next to Don Heinrich, our backup quarterback. I leaned over and whispered to him, "Who the hell is that?"

"That's Vince Lombardi," he answered. "And you'll know him soon enough."

On other teams, particularly in high school and college ball, there was a clear delegation of skills: the players were responsible for physical ability alone, and we relied on the coaches to understand strategy. When you sat down to learn a play, the coach told you what your task was—where you were to start, where you were to end up, and what you were responsible for in between—and then you went onto the field to develop whatever physical abilities were needed to get that job done. Half the time you didn't even need to worry about what the other players were up to. You learned your part of the play, you did your job, and you hoped everything happened according to plan.

Tom Landry and Vince Lombardi unlocked a whole new level of the game for me, and for all of us on the Giants. They knew that for the team to work as one connected, responsive unit, each player had to understand *why* he was doing what he was doing. It wasn't enough for us to know our individual patterns; we also were expected to know how our movement affected the movement of all the other players on the field, and ultimately how it all added up to a play that would work. We were expected to understand *why* we would outplay the other team if we followed Lombardi or Landry's instructions.

When I was playing with the Cardinals, a strategy session for me was something that I just had to get through so I could go out on the field and play. When a coach would start to put a play up on the board, I'd think, "Here we go again. Same thing I've seen fifty thousand times before." Suddenly, when I arrived at the Giants' training camp for the first time, I discovered that so much was possible that I had been missing. The equipment was newer, more state-of-the-art; the locker rooms were cleaner; the trainers were more knowledgeable; and practices were better organized and more punctual.

I think the players on the Cardinals were every bit as athletically gifted as those on the Giants, but the crucial difference was that Lombardi and Landry insisted that players understand strategy, not just execute it. So that meant that they made their picks for brains as well as for brawn. The Giants were the smartest team I ever played with, and probably the smartest team the league has ever seen. Lombardi and Landry would allow some leeway if you made a physical error on the field, or if you just didn't have the strength, stamina, or agility to get the job done. But if you made one too many mental errors, you wouldn't last more than a few games. It wouldn't be long before you were traded or just plain cut.

As I got to know the Giants' way of doing things better, I gradually came to realize that the Cardinals had a reputation in the NFL for being a classless organization and for not spending enough money to win . . . not that I didn't already have an inkling of that already. Take Dick Nolan, for instance, who was part of the same trade deal as I was. He spent one year with the Cardinals and then got traded back to the Giants. When he got back, we had many conversations about how terrible things were in Chicago with the Cardinals. He was glad to get back to New York—let's put it that way. I remember once, not too long after the start of the '58 season, when I was warming up with the Giants to play against the Cardinals, their owner, Billy Bidwell, came up to me and said something like, "Why didn't you get in that kind of shape when you were playing with us?" I kept the true answer to myself, but I knew that any improvements I'd made were due to the quality of the Giants' coaching.

For the first time ever, when I started playing for Lombardi and Landry, I realized that I was looking forward to defensive and offensive meetings. Unlike the other players, I was going to both units' meetings so I could play either side if they needed me, and that meant I saw both Lombardi and Landry every day, sometimes twice a day. They were the two most engaging, dynamic teachers I'd ever had. The goal for both of them was the same: we had to know *why* we were doing what we were doing. But their methods of getting to that goal couldn't have been more different.

Lombardi was a live wire. I can't remember a single meeting when he didn't break the chalk on the board putting up a play. But it wasn't all about show; the man knew what he was talking about like no offensive coordinator I had ever known. His plays were precise down to the length of the first step the offensive end should take to achieve his block and how he should time it so it was executed just as the quarterback began his first step away from center and out of the path of the pulling guards.

We didn't question a word Lombardi said. He was the one who asked the questions. If he sensed that our attention had drifted, or even if he knew he had us hanging on his every word, he'd surprise us out of the blue with a question. "What are you going to do if the guard counters in this direction instead of that one?" We had to be on our toes, because we couldn't answer his questions if we hadn't understood the play in its entirety. And if he ever truly stumped us, if he suggested a scenario that no one could think of a way out of or through, he had a favorite saying. "Well, in that case," he'd say, "you'd react like a football player."

Landry's style in the classroom was much less dynamic. He was almost like a schoolteacher: completely matter-of-fact and straightforward. He had earned a degree in industrial engineering from the University of Houston, and he had expected engineering to be his life's work. I don't think he ever expected to be the coach of the Cowboys for twenty-nine years. In the classroom, we could see the engineer in him. My guess is that he often thought of the players as numbers and symbols in an equation he was challenged to solve.

That single-minded focus made Landry a much less warm person than Lombardi, but at the same time, his lack of emotionality made him more approachable. We never dared ask Lombardi a question, but we felt comfortable enough to ask Landry for clarification. The catch was that if we ever voiced doubt, Landry would go to great lengths to explain why we were wrong and he was right. And his proofs were always so irrefutable that we were left almost as reluctant to speak up as in Lombardi's meetings. If Lombardi allowed for variables by telling us to react like football players, Landry saw no room for deviation. He'd finish a lecture by saying, "And if you do it my way, we'll win." Most of the time, we did.

Lombardi and Landry simply insisted on a higher level of precise thinking than any other coaches out there. On the Cardinals, as I've mentioned, I had to chase the ball around myself if I wanted to practice kicking. And during a game, if a holder set the ball down for me the wrong way, laces forward . . . well, I just had to kick the laces. That kind of thing never happened on the Giants. Landry made sure that the center knew exactly how many times the ball had to spin between leaving his hand and being caught by the quarterback, so that when he put it on the ground, the laces would be facing away from me. That was the level of precision—and professionalism between teammates—that we were held to.

To be honest, I didn't know the Giants actually worked on their kicking until I got to camp in Salem. But suddenly I realized that I'd be having scheduled kicking practices—and people to work with me. Landry was the kicking coach, and he paid attention to every kick and every detail of what I was doing. We kickers had two-a-days, so every day we got up early. One big difference from the Cardinals' training camp was that at Willamette University, where the Giants had their training camp, we had to show up for all three meals and sign in. With the Cardinals, if you didn't want to eat at the cafeteria, you didn't have to show up to eat. After breakfast, I would head out first to practice kicking with Landry, and the rest of the team would come out fifteen minutes later.

The kickers would start at the twenty-five-yard line, kick ten or so times, move back ten yards, kick, and move back another ten yards until we were fifty yards out. We would kick only two or three times then—Landry knew how much that took out of your leg. It's better for placekickers today since they outlawed the tee, because it's less strenuous. Landry used to say to me, "If you get tired, you'll start bad habits, and it doesn't do anybody any good to practice bad habits."

During the season I always worked on kicking with the same center, Ray Wietecha, and the same holder, Charlie Conerly, who was the quarterback and an artist when it came to holding. He was one of the best; he would put his finger down and say, "I'm going to put the ball right here," so that I could line up to that spot where he said he was going to put the ball, and that's where he would put it. I never saw the laces when Conerly held for me. But he wouldn't hold for anyone unless he was sure that guy was good enough to make the team, so when I first got to training camp, I worked with a backup holder. The center, Ray Wietecha, was the same way: he wouldn't snap for you unless he thought you would make the team. I knew in the back of my mind that if Conerly and Wietecha agreed to practice with me, I could be pretty sure that things were going to work out with the Giants.

I went out to Salem not sure if I would make the team and with doubts about whether I was good enough as a kicker. But being able to both kick and play was a bonus. One of the other kickers, a kid from Ohio State, was my main competition during camp. Mostly, what he did was kick—he also played backup defensive back, but not very well—and even then I could see that I was a better kicker, with better range and more strength.

I also knew that the team wasn't happy with their current kicker, Ben Agajanian. He only focused on kicking, and he only flew in on the weekends to practice or play games—he wanted to stay in California with his family the rest of the time. I could sense that his attitude didn't fit with the Giants' level of dedication, and they were ready for someone new.

I remember one morning, toward the end of training camp, the other players were watching from the sidelines as the kickers finished up our practice. By that time I'd already been working with Conerly and Wietecha for a while. I made a successful kick, and suddenly the team started to sing "Bye Bye Agie" to that teasing, sarcastic melody that ends with "We hate to see you go." Agie, of course, wasn't at camp when they sang that song, but I'm sure the word got back to him. That's when I knew that the team had accepted me.

But that was only the first step. The fact was that on the Giants, we played for our coaches' approval as much as we played to win. Everybody could sense that we had something special in Lombardi and Landry. No one on that team had ever been coached in a way that could even compare to Lombardi and Landry's expertise. Even the head coach, Jim Lee Howell, had the sense to recognize the extraordinary talent he had in his assistant coaches, and he largely stepped aside and allowed them to run the show. He was the man who kept practices running on time, who kept us in line with the pocket watch he carried. But he left the coaching to Lombardi and Landry. Some players said that if you passed the coaches' office late at night, you'd likely catch a glimpse of Lombardi and Landry viewing and reviewing game footage, while Howell would be stretched out on the couch reading the paper.

Howell's instinct was right, and it's to his credit that he was willing to acknowledge the talent he had working under him. A lesser coach might not have. But the thing is that both Lombardi and Landry commanded such respect that it would be tough to ever think ill of them. As much as we all craved their approval, and as little as we got it, I never heard anyone on the team say a bad thing about either man. There were players on defense who could get a little edgy, because you simply never knew where you stood with Landry. Praise was rarely forthcoming from either of them, but Landry especially was impossible to read. If you made an error, you'd know it, and you'd see it over and over again on the game film at the next meeting. But if you did something right . . . well, that was the way it was supposed to be. There was nothing left to say about it.

I'm sure none of us ever emerged from a film-reviewing session with Lombardi or Landry unscathed. If we played a Sunday game, we'd have Monday off, and first thing Tuesday, we'd look at the tapes of the game. Usually, after playing a game, I'd have a whole list of opinions: "I really think I did this well," and "I hope they didn't notice that I made that error." Without a doubt, they *would* notice the errors, and on top of that, most of the things I thought I'd done well wouldn't look quite so good on tape. More often than not, the coaches could point out how our successes were more due to the opponent making an error than anything else. They could pick you apart. And they did. Often I left those Tuesday meetings thinking, "I've got to do better, because I can't go through another session like that." Playing for the Giants took far more mental toughness than it did physical toughness. And I think that's what set us apart.

What made me successful in that kind of demanding atmosphere was that the Giants accepted me as a player as well as a kicker. Most kickers today are ostracized and not part of the team. They have their own private practice at a separate place from the rest of the team. My situation was totally different. The Giants needed somebody who wanted to be part of the team. Not too long into training camp that first season, I started to realize that the guys *wanted* me to make the team—I constantly got the feeling that they were all pulling for me. This was, needless to say, like night and day compared to the Cardinals, where everyone was constantly looking over their shoulders.

Instead of dreading going to practice, I enjoyed camp. The two-a-days were hard work, but the revelation that the Giants were serious about scoring with field goals made it all worth it. Other teams scoffed at getting three points for a trip down the field. Maybe they didn't consider field goals manly enough. The Giants certainly did. When I pulled a quadriceps muscle, I was anxious to get back into the competition after only a few days of rest and ice, because I wanted to be a part of everything. I looked forward to certain drills because it was a chance to show what I could do.

I think the reason we were sent all the way to Oregon for training was so that nobody in New York could read about who was excelling and who was doing poorly. They would have no idea how good we were or how bad we were and had no way to track who was getting cut, who was out of shape, and so on. Now the teams all train somewhere close by the area in which they play and there is no escaping the media anymore. But back then, we didn't have much contact with broadcasters. As a kicker, they knew what I did, so I didn't have *any* contact with them at all. They didn't visit the locker room or go to practices regularly. They weren't allowed in, for one thing, and they usually didn't have time because they had other jobs during the week. Chris Schenkel broadcast the Giants games on television in '58 but he didn't live in New York, so the only contact we'd have with him would be before games, when he would come in and say hello.

The absence of any media presence allowed us to focus totally on our training. And that meant almost constant hard work. The older guys knew what was coming and accepted it as part of building a successful program. Veterans such as Frank Gifford and Kyle Rote went through the motions of camp just like the rest of us, although they knew they were already on the team. Seeing them work so hard and enjoy it had a powerful effect on the rest of us. We knew we all had to do it to be successful. In those days, once the season was over, most veterans never worked out until training camp began. We had six preseason games, as opposed to the four they have today, and the games, along with the practices, were primarily to get us into shape and get us used to the knocks we'd be taking.

We did something called the "Nutcracker" during practice, which definitely got us prepared for the beating we might get on the field. To execute the Nutcracker, we had two dummies that we put about five feet apart. We then got an offensive player and a defensive player. The offensive player was supposed to block the defensive player. The offensive player had a back behind him, to whom he would give the ball. Then the back would have to try to run through the hole between the dummies created by the offensive player blocking the defensive player. There were some guys who were pretty good at the Nutcracker yet still got really embarrassed on defense in that drill, because the offensive guys would just overpower them. It was a tough drill and we had advance notice when we were going to do it in practice.

Camp wasn't all about physical training, either. Every year during training camp, we had a visit from the commissioner of the NFL, Bert Bell. He'd discuss how to talk to broadcasters, how to dress for a road trip, gambling, and calling the league office or him to discuss any issues that might arise during the season. But neither he nor any of the coaches on the Giants' staff ever addressed us about our personal lives. That was something we were expected to sort out on our own, no matter how much time we were called upon to be away for games. They gave us free time before and after meetings or practices when we could write letters or call our families, but I didn't call my wife too often. For one thing, it wasn't cheap to call Florida from Oregon, and there was only one phone in the dormitory hall. It seemed like it was always in use at every free moment we had, with several guys lined up to use it next.

Kathy and I had that tough period while we were still in Chicago, where she was trying to raise our kids in a hotel and under awful conditions. But when I left for Giants training camp, I was sure that there was still hope for our marriage, and as soon as I saw what things were like with my new team, I wrote to let her know that life would be different. However, I wasn't a very good letter writer and neither was she. Frankly, I also don't think I was that much in love at that point in my life. So there weren't too many calls back home.

But football was starting to matter for me again and was consuming more and more of my passion and energy. There was hardly any time to think about anything else, and it was hard to believe that just the season before, I had been willing to consider retiring from pro ball. Now I was kicking better than all the competition and had been accepted into the fraternity of players. After practice, they'd ask me to go along with them when they went out to get some beers or sodas. We didn't have our own cars there, but some of the team members had made friends with the locals and had use of their cars. Somebody would nonchalantly ask me if I was driving today or tell me it was my turn to buy a round of whatever we were drinking, and that's when I knew I was in with the players and on the team.

It was like being accepted into any group. It's an incredibly satisfying feeling once you realize that you can help them along to their goal, that you can contribute, and that the coaches and owners think so, too. There's nothing like being accepted by your peers and being part of a group. Retired NFL players often say that's what they miss the most—not the playing or the practices, but the camaraderie. And when your peers are the New York Giants, with players such as Kyle Rote and Charlie Conerly, people who have championship titles and know what it takes to win—well, for a football player, it doesn't get much better than that.

CHAPTER 4

"Try to Win Every Game"

There's a saying, "Once a Giant, always a Giant." More than fifty years after I played my first game with them, I know that saying still rings true. From the moment I showed up at training camp in the summer of 1958, I knew that I had stumbled upon something different, something great, and that feeling stayed with me for the rest of my life. Even today, I can't watch a Giants game without getting swept up in my passion for the team.

At the opening of the new Cowboys Stadium on September 20, 2009, the Cowboys played the Giants. I was the guest of Cowboys owner Jerry Jones and sat with him, my old broadcasting colleague John Madden, and former president George W. Bush and his wife, Laura. I had never seen anything like that stadium. There was a regular-season record crowd—105,000-plus fans, more than any in NFL history. It was the biggest crowd ever to see a sporting event in Texas, which is quite an accomplishment. As you know, football is very big there.

Looking down at the field from far above, the incredible size and scale of the stadium left a part of me wishing I was with the Giants right then. They were about to play a game in the world's largest domed stadium, with a retractable roof and a video screen that stretches from one twenty-yard line to the other. But I had my time long ago, and now I can only imagine what it must be like to play football in a place like that.

Of course, you can't root too hard for the Giants when you're sitting next to Jerry Jones. Jones knows everybody and is always surrounded by friends, so it was not surprising to me that we had front-row seats that day, or that we were next to President and Mrs. Bush. We all talked about how many turnovers the Cowboys had and the way the game was progressing, instantly at ease in the world of football. The president is a real sports fan and could talk about pass patterns and intricate strategy questions that I wouldn't expect most fans to be aware of, but he was. I inquired into how he was filling his spare time and he said, "I don't have any spare time." He was making several speeches in the area and working on his book. So we went back to talking strictly about sports, and the president tried to include his wife as much as he could. She was very nice and even more attractive in person than she is on television. Jones, on the other hand, stayed very much involved in the game, eternally focused on the performance of his players.

Gradually I got more and more caught up in the game and managed to forget about the grandeur of the setting. Pretty soon all that mattered was what was happening on the field—and I could tell the players felt the same way. It can be intimidating for a visiting team coming into that stadium, although the Cowboys would say it's inspirational. It certainly didn't seem to intimidate the Giants that much, but then again, once a game starts, good players learn to shut out their awareness of the surroundings, the crowd, anything except what's happening in front of them.

Ever since I got into broadcasting, I've learned that when I watch a game, I have to try to hide my enthusiasm and how hard I'm rooting, although people usually know who I'm for. So sitting there in the new Cowboys Stadium, I had mixed emotions seeing my old team play. Every time I watch them, I think about what I would do or could do under their circumstances. That day, they won against the Cowboys on a field goal at the last second.

I couldn't help wondering how it would feel to still be able to accomplish something like that.

I drifted back, as I have so many times, to memories of 1958.

After training camp broke up, we went into the preseason, where I knew the real test of my abilities would come. We had to play our six preseason games in remote locations: Portland, Oregon; Salt Lake City; Louisville; a baseball park in Newark; Syracuse; and Bangor, Maine. The conditions in those stadiums were less than ideal. It was almost like being back with the Cardinals again. Nothing was on par with what the Giants were used to: Yankee Stadium.

I had played in Yankee Stadium as a visitor with the Cardinals, and we thought it was a palace. The locker rooms were pristine. Everybody had a big locker, a place for their mail, and a place to put their shoes. Chicago was a low-rent operation, and all of a sudden I was back to playing in low-rent surroundings. Because we were playing preseason games, we had to make do with what was there, and it was not pleasant. Our first game was at Multnomah Stadium in Portland, not too far from our training camp in Salem. I think the stadium was also for baseball, because they didn't sod the infield, and we had to play on dirt.

In Bangor, Maine, where we played the Packers, we didn't have any closets in the hotel we stayed at, the Penobscot Hotel. Whatever clothes we had at training camp had to come with us, because we weren't going back to camp, so we had to hang everything on the exposed heating pipes in the room. There was no air-conditioning, and the whole place felt very primitive. There were no lockers in the locker rooms, either, just a nail to hang our uniforms on.

We played in a municipal stadium in Louisville because John Unitas of the Colts, the team we played against there, had gone to college in the city. Teams often scheduled exhibition games with the hope that a local crowd, uninterested in pro football, might come out to see a former college or high school player. The strategy failed as often as it worked, though. To make matters worse, the state fair had just departed from the area, and there was elephant dung on the field when we played.

Sometimes it felt as if our exhibition games were more of an obligation for our fans than a pleasure. There were very few sellouts. Most of the towns we went to took sort of a puzzled attitude toward us. The prevailing question was, "What are the Giants doing here?" The NFL still hadn't caught on in popularity, so it was entirely possible for us to come, play our exhibition game, and leave without the majority of the town even knowing we had been there.

We had a charter plane and flew from Portland to Salt Lake City, where we played the 49ers. Our first-round draft choice was from Utah, Lee Grosscup, and he was one of the reasons we went back to his hometown. Ownership wanted to display him there— but ironically, I don't remember that he even got in the game.

Even in those conditions, I was plenty excited to finally be playing actual games with the Giants. Everything—from the fit of the uniforms to the way the organization was run—was so much smoother than it had been on the Cardinals that I felt eternally privileged. I was grateful just to be there, and I wanted to prove myself. At the time, there was no limit to the number of players a team could take to training camp, so we had about a hundred players and limited playing time. When I was out there, I knew I had better do something. Even though they were preseason games, I still had to perform.

The biggest fear of any player during training camp and the preseason, of course, is getting cut. This is just as true whether you're an established veteran, a raw recruit, or someone like me, who came in a trade. If the Grim Reaper, the Turk, or whatever the players called him doesn't visit and ask you to come with him and bring your playbook, you make the assumption, "Okay, I made the team." You count how many are left and if you're one of thirty-three, then you made the team. I was one of the last men standing.

I remember a tremendous sense of relief when I realized I was safe, and I could sense that everybody was treating me differently, like I was one of them. Those who were on the borderline, or "on the bubble," as they say, didn't really get accepted into the group, so when I felt the noticeable shift between being on the outside and being on the inside, it was like a very real weight had been lifted from my shoulders.

It's usually an assistant coach who's tasked with being the Turk—the bearer of bad news for the guys who would be cut. Jim Lee Howell, the head coach, had that job with the Giants, making him one of the very rare head coaches who shouldered that most unpleasant responsibility. I was close to some of the fellows who got cut; a couple of times it was my roommate of the moment. There would be a knock at the door, and we'd open it with trepidation. Coach Howell would come in and say he wanted to see my roommate and he'd tell him to bring his playbook . . . and then he was gone. When the coach knocked and called for my roommate instead of me, it felt like death passing me over.

The preseason was crucial because we didn't have all the off-season programs that players have today to help them stay in good physical condition and to allow them to display what they can do. We just weren't in as good shape as players are today; in fact, I'd go so far as to say that players today don't really need training camp. They all do it, but they don't really need it. Most of the players live in the town where they play, so the stadium training facilities are open to them; it's almost like having their own health club. They can work out whenever they want to, although plenty of them don't take advantage of that. But back in those days, we played preseason games to get in shape, because almost everybody had an off-season job that didn't involve sports of any kind, so we had to play ourselves into football condition, as well as exhibit whatever talent we had.

We were in those antiquated, second-rate facilities and had to turn out first-rate performances. That's pressure . . . and believe me, we felt it. In a lot of cases, the grass on the field was not good, so getting traction was a challenge, as was finding a decent place to kick from. As I mentioned, they had outlawed the tee by the time I was playing with the Giants. I had to kick the ball right off the ground, and in some of the places we went, the grass was either nonexistent or it was too long. It was like hitting a golf ball out of the rough. But whether I liked it or not, my career hinged on those kicks.

Lombardi and Landry were involved with us daily during the preseason. They took the games very seriously, but they also recognized them as an opportunity to try new things and take risks they might not gamble on during the regular season. They used the preseason as an opportunity to incorporate new ideas they had during the off-season into the offense and the defense.

Both of them had a way of presenting their new ideas that made them seem incredibly vital and important. Lombardi, for instance, would say, "This is going to be our bread and butter," and "This is the play we're going to use the entire season," and "This is a play that we have to make work." Many years later, I had a rare glimpse into exactly how Lombardi felt about what a crucial opportunity the preseason is for teams. It's one of my favorite memories of Lombardi, and I think it captures perfectly the way he coached and lived.

It was only shortly after I'd begun broadcasting with CBS, and I was having lunch with Bill MacPhail, who was the head of CBS Sports. We ran into Lombardi and Harland Svare, a former Giants player who'd just become coach of the Los Angeles Rams, and they joined us at our table. The Rams had fallen on hard times, and Svare was asking us about how we thought he should approach the exhibition season. Should he be out to win every game? Or should he be more concerned with watching and evaluating players?

This was during the days of competition between the CBS and NBC networks, and between the AFL and the NFL. So Bill MacPhail immediately cut in and said, "We can't let them beat us on the field, or they're going to start beating us in the ratings. I hope you win every game; we've got to try for it."

He started getting more and more animated, so I said, "Bill, you're getting excited about it. Take it easy."

Just then, Lombardi jabbed his finger into my chest.

"Son," he said, "he should try to win every game. He's got to believe in his heart that he should win every game. If you don't believe in your heart that you're playing to win, you should be in another business."

He almost stuck his finger through my chest when he said it. By the time he got through with me, I was ready to go back out and play myself. I'll never forget it.

Landry was just as tough about the preseason as Lombardi. He was a pretty imposing man himself, standing about 6–1 or 6–2 and weighing about 210 pounds. In his football-playing days, he was a force to contend with. I have no personal experience of playing against him, but I remember guys talking about how Landry was hard-hitting. When he shifted into coaching, he insisted on his players developing the same hard-hitting style, and he used training camp and the preseason to hammer it into us.

I heard that when he went on to be head coach of the Cowboys, he'd open their training camp with what was known as the "Landry Mile." The players had to run a mile in fewer than six minutes, and Landry would do it himself. If you couldn't run it, I suppose the consequences depended on who you were. If you were Bob Lilly or someone like that and you didn't make the time, you weren't going to be cut. I know some of the big names, who were supposed to be in great shape, such as Tony Dorsett, didn't make the prescribed time.

Landry was a punter himself in the NFL, so of course he was my kicking coach. He approached kicking like an engineer—systematically and scientifically. When I worked with Landry during practice, if I missed in one direction, he would say, "Well, this is what happened . . ." and he'd identify exactly how the movement of my kick had led the ball off course. He would tell me, "Keep your head down"; "Remember your straight follow-through"; and "Lock your ankle," which is hard to do. He would tell me how far to stand away from the ball to get the most effective result (a step and a half). I would step first with my kicking foot, then take a long stride with my left foot, and then swing my right leg, like it was a club, through the ball. We worked on my kicking for ten or fifteen minutes a day throughout the entire season, but it was during the preseason that he really drilled me.

There were some days when I had a lot of power and punch and some days when I didn't. Usually the reason had to do with timing, and he would spot that pretty quickly. He would say things such as, "Your first step wasn't long enough so you weren't getting power through the ball," and we would fix it. I'd never had any kind of kicking coaching like that before. I'd sort of fallen into kicking at the University of Arkansas. The coaches had said that anyone who thought he could kick should come out fifteen minutes early and try out. I did a better job than anyone they had currently kicking, and that's how I got started. I just wanted to go out and try. I had fooled around kicking with a buddy in high school, but we had a guy on the team who was better than I was, although he didn't end up going into professional sports.

Working with Landry, I knew I got better with my kicking, but to be honest, that first preseason, I was never in awe of him. Landry wasn't Landry yet; he was just a great kicking coach who told me what to do.

Landry had a reputation for being cold and reserved. As a matter of fact, he wasn't particularly critical, but more practical and analytical. If he realized I was having an off day, he would just say, "It's one of those days." I finally learned over time that I'd just never know where I stood with him. I remember thinking, "There's no pleasing this guy!" I think the average coach, at some point or another, will say something encouraging, even just a "Good job" or "Good work" if a player is doing well. I don't remember Landry ever saying to anybody that they were playing well. He did say about Bob Lilly, "There's only one Bob Lilly." That was the ultimate compliment from Landry—and it only fell to the most deserving. To me, as an observer, Bob Lilly seemed almost like a man among boys, like Jim Brown as a fullback was a huge guy and almost impossible to block.

Landry's reservedness was often a topic of locker room discussions. He treated all the guys the same—no one ever really knew where he stood. I don't know why he was that way; I guess it was just his temperament. Early in the preseason, the veteran players warned me not to take it personally. I talked with Andy Robustelli and players who were regulars on the defensive unit who played for Landry, such as Sam Huff. I'd ask them, "How do you know if you're doing well?" and their answer was that I'd never know. I'd just have to try to please him, and I'd know from the praise of my teammates and from others what I was doing right. Landry was a revered father figure, and you would feel embarrassed if you misbehaved in front of him.

Even though Landry was sparse with the compliments, everybody who played or kicked for him wanted to emulate the way he was. As I said, he lived by the maxim of "faith, family, and football," but of course my first introduction to him was through the game, so it was only gradually that I began to see how he honored God and home. I would discover, ultimately, that it was with the same reverence, the same total commitment with which he approached coaching. People don't know that when one of his players was severely injured in an away game, Coach Landry would typically stay behind after the game for a day or two to be with that player in the hospital. He didn't want press coverage for acts like that, and he made sure those things weren't publicized.

Landry's Christian beliefs were very strong, and even though he never talked about them, we knew it. He lived his beliefs, but he never really brought them up. I don't remember anyone telling me about his religion or how it affected his life. We were just aware of it and saw that he lived what he taught and believed. We played our games on Sundays, of course, so I didn't see him go to church, but I know he made time. Like anything else, if you want to get it done, you make time to get it done.

We knew, of course, that he had a very good-looking wife and was a devoted family man. We knew by watching his actions around the rest of the team and during the off-hours, when he was with his kids and wife, how deeply his devotion ran through him. After the games, when we went to parties, he didn't drink and would stay apart from anyone getting raucous. Even when we weren't up to anything questionable, Landry mostly kept himself apart. We had no social activity with him. From time to time, outside of practice, we might run into him in the hall or in the elevator of the building near Yankee Stadium where he and many of the players, myself included, lived during the season. But the extent of the conversation would be, "Evening, Coach," and maybe a nod in return. There was no such thing as small talk from Landry.

· · ·

I often wonder how Lombardi and Landry would have coached today's kind of football. The game has evolved in significant ways; sometimes it seems like a new sport. I think perhaps the most extreme difference is that player limits are higher nowadays, so teams can afford specialists. They can have a guy whose only job is, say, to cover the slot receiver, and they can use him on third downs and long yardage. Back then, we couldn't have specialists like that because of the limit on the number of players we could have. I believe the so-called increased complexity of the game today is due solely to the fact that coaches can substitute and rely on specialists.

That kind of specialization has also carried over into the way teams are coached. The Giants had five coaches when I was there, including Lombardi and Landry. And in actuality, it was more like having four coaches, because our head coach, as I've said, was less involved with football strategy than with administrative duties. Nowadays, the Dallas Cowboys have twenty assistant coaches. Each position has a coach, whereas for us, Lombardi ran the whole offense and Landry ran the whole defense. We did have an end coach, because as a tight end, which I was, you're involved in blocking and pass receiving. We also had an assistant line coach who answered to Landry.

In the beginning of practice, the tight ends would go off on one side of the field, the defensive backs would go over with Landry, and then the whole defense would be there working with him and synchronizing everything. The assistant line coach would take the offensive linemen and work on their techniques, and then we would all come together. So essentially we had four clumps of people, each working on their own thing. At that time, one field was sufficient for us to practice on; now teams use three fields.

For my money, I'm not sure the increasing number of coaches and complexity is worth it. All those coaches sometimes just get in one another's way. It's hard to forget that unfortunate episode in Houston when Buddy Ryan punched his fellow assistant coach Kevin Gilbride on the sidelines. That is an extreme case, but in reality, it's hard to get twenty guys on the same page, even when each has a clear, specific assignment. And to make matters even more embroiled, there's no regulation on coaching staffs. There is no cap on how many assistants a team can have or how much it can pay them. Although teams can't be competitive by spending more on players than other teams or by having more players, they can compete with how many coaches they have and how much specializing they do.

The increasing complexity just keeps radiating outward, from the players to the coaches and even to the broadcasting. Modern announcers have gotten exponentially more technical in their analyses. You have three guys stepping all over one another, throwing a little bull, and describing things on such a technical level that the audience at home can have a hard time following them. I know some fans who love sinking their teeth into the technical side of the game, but for a lot of people at home, the point is just to watch the ball and go along for the ride. I remember John Madden saying to me once, "If they ever understand what the hell we're talking about, we've got a problem."

Another big difference between football today and back then was that we had nothing approaching the level of scrutiny that players such as Tony Romo go through. Our relationship with writers and the rest of the media was so different. They traveled with us on the train or plane and became our friends. They wouldn't dare write anything personally negative about us. If somebody got drunk on the train, which happened quite often, it just wasn't reported.

There were a couple of guys on the *New York Times* who got to be good friends of mine and they never wrote anything other than a favorable personal comment about any of us. I think it was partly due to a sense of friendship. That feeling of togetherness trumped the feeling of "I have to get a story. I have to write something. If I dig up dirt, I better use it." Relations with the media were simpler because they followed the team line as well. Whatever the team wanted them to say about our personal lives or our team ethos is what they said.

Somebody somewhere down the line, however, thought that the newspaper ought to pay for the reporters' transportation instead of the team. They felt that reporters became obligated to the team, because the owners were picking up the checks for their meals, their accommodations on the road, their transportation, almost everything. The way reporting was done was also a lot different. There were no television or radio reporters traveling with us in the beginning, and nobody with a recorder on him. About the time I quit playing, there got to be more newspapers and radio stations covering the team. Talk radio really sparked people to come up with something wrong and uncover scandals, such as So-and-So's running around on his wife or, as the years went on, So-and-So is hooked on performance-enhancing drugs. Reporters began to feel that their foremost responsibility was not to the team but to the fans. Then they went a step forward to feeling that their foremost responsibility was to entice people to read their paper or to watch their program. That's when the media became ubiquitous and started heavily following players and reporting on every detail of their careers as well as their personal lives.

One of the effects of the media frenzy surrounding football is favoritism. There are major stars who are practically deified by the press, the public, and—to the detriment of the game—by their coaches. Back in my day there were, of course, stars. There always have been, and there always will be; it's part of the fun of the game. But Lombardi and Landry never got involved in playing favorites. They knew it poisoned the integrity of the game.

When they evaluated the films and the plays of each group, neither coach spared anyone. In Lombardi's meetings Frank Gifford got treated no differently than a backup offensive back. There were no favorites; he chewed everybody out. Too often nowadays, coaches leave their star players alone and just chew out those who are dispensable. When that happens, to survive, players have to develop a group that helps them defend themselves and ward off the critical things the coach might say—I know we did that with the Cardinals, and I think it happens in a lot of cases today. When coaches are too awed by star players, it creates resentment among everybody else. You end up practically having two opposing teams wearing the same colors, like what happened to the Cowboys in 2008 with Terrell Owens. He had a group of followers, and he was very vocal in his criticism of the play-calling and the favoritism of Tony Romo, and the Cowboys developed a divided locker room as a result. It became almost impossible for them to win.

This is just one more reason why the complexity of coaching staffs today doesn't work. Having twenty assistant coaches can really exacerbate a lack of team unity and philosophy. Each coach starts defending his own people, and the team ends up being divided by groups and by criticism. If a player feels singled out as the culprit, his position coach will jump in to try to defend him, and it turns into a never-ending drama. In conversations before, during, and after Bible study, they start defending their method of teaching, the techniques of their players, their positions, whatever it might be. Usually somebody will remind them that we're here for Bible study, but then they'll start using Bible passages as justifications of their methods or how their players are performing.

If a Lombardi or a Landry were to come back to coach in today's world, they wouldn't want to have twenty assistant coaches. They would probably have one or two, as Landry did when coaching here in Dallas and as Lombardi did when he went to Green Bay. When there is too much repetition and not enough to do, the head coach invents things for them to do, telling them to break down films or saying, "Teach this guy to do such-and-such this way," when the player maybe does it his own way, but does it well. They have him use their technique instead of his own, which has been successful, for no reason.

Part of what made Lombardi and Landry so successful back then was that they didn't have their message filtered down through numerous supporting staff. They largely let the players play. They didn't make robots of them. They didn't make them fit their system. For them, it was about seeing who they had and building around what was already in place, as opposed to distorting things to fit into their philosophy. It was an approach that was more flexible than the view most coaches adhere to today.

Both Lombardi and Landry would pay attention when players lucked into a play that was successful. If a player did something spontaneously or even accidentally and got a good result, they would adopt it and allow players to follow through with that new idea. Lombardi in particular had an eye for accidents. If we were running a play in practice and someone blew a pattern or hit somebody by mistake, Lombardi might say, "Wait a minute, let's look at that again." Sometimes we'd end up with a great new play because Lombardi had zeroed in on what anybody else would have thought of as a failure, and he had seen how it could be made to work regularly. And he'd listen to us players, too, if we came up with an idea or if we thought of a physically easier way to accomplish a play. We just had to go to him and say, "Hey, I think this might work." He'd look it over, and most of the time he'd be willing to incorporate it if it truly was functional. The second time we beat the Cleveland Browns in '58, we beat them with a play that developed in practice by accident.

Though Landry was willing to discuss his own plays with us at length, until he was satisfied we'd understood them, he didn't openly seek our suggestions. It was tougher to go to him with ideas—you had to sort of gird your loins to talk to the man. He was somewhat flexible, but overall pretty set in his ways. At the same time, players at least had a chance to talk to him about ideas. Today, with twenty assistant coaches, it's close to impossible for players to get a new idea up the chain of command. In coaches' ideas today, players' opinions have very little merit.

As much as I would like to see the old system of coaching restored, I don't think there are many head coaches who would have the guts to make the change. Tom Coughlin in New York or Bill Belichick in New England might have the courage to do something like that, but otherwise, head coaches don't tend to question the accepted standard that you have to have a coach for every position. Someone like Coughlin or Belichick might have the courage to go back and say, "I have enough knowledge to do this. Let's be more of a team." On the other hand, they would be subjecting themselves to an absurd, unwanted amount of scrutiny and aggravation were they to implement a change like that. The media would put them through the wringer for it. They would declare it inconceivable to operate a team without specialized personnel, down to a position such as "offensive quality control." (Apparently this person's sole job description is to analyze videos and create tendency reports to give to the offensive coordinators, making him kind of like an advance scout.)

Of course, in a way, coaching styles have *had* to change drastically over the past few decades, due to the advent of video. When Lombardi and Landry first became coaches, there was no such thing as videotape. Everything was done on film. If the Giants' opponent of the week didn't have film or didn't turn it over to us, Lombardi and Landry couldn't analyze how to break it down. A lot of cheating and nepotism developed out of the limitations of film. Sometimes we had film access we weren't supposed to have. Assistant coaches who had buddies on other staffs would get a copy of the film and send it over to us. I'm sure other teams did the same thing.

For those teams who didn't have the connections to get off-limits film, they had to depend on their advance scout and his appraisal of the opponent. It got to be that if a team had a good scout who gave you a realistic appraisal, you had a big advantage. The Giants had a guy named Jack Lavelle who was a very good scout. He would go to opposing games the previous week and come back with an evaluation of their personnel, their tendencies, what their strong points were—all in minute detail. In terms of advance scouting, we had an advantage. Now everything is on video and teams have an obligation to swap video, so there is no more cheating . . . in that department, at least. Coaches will always try to find ways to create an advantage for their team.

I remember the 2008 controversy when Brett Favre had a long talk with a coach who was an opponent of the Packers. And of course we've all heard that when a player from one team goes to another team, the coaches of his new team will pick his brain to learn their opponent's automatics, snap count, and cadence. I'm sure that still goes on, but to be honest, I think it's pretty harmless. I don't think that drilling a new player for information has that great a value. Too many times, a player who is traded to another team doesn't know his former teammates as players well and doesn't know their strong points. He knows the praise they get, but he doesn't know what their tendencies are. He doesn't pay that much attention to his own team. The atmosphere centers around "who I'm playing next week." What one's own teammates can do—that gets ignored.

I have to believe, even with all these modern shifts and the very real advantages of videotape, that teams these days are hobbled by being overcoached. Lombardi and Landry, were they to coach in today's world, would just come in and clean up. The game hasn't passed them by; it's simply different, but not necessarily better. In 2009, Bobby Knight asked me if Lombardi would be successful today, and I told him definitively, "Lombardi and Landry would be successful in any era."

CHAPTER 5

"Training Doesn't End with Training Camp"

The preseason had been the final test. By the end, we all knew our place was secure: we were Giants. But Lombardi and Landry were teachers at heart, and good teachers never stop teaching. Training camp and preseason were about building our confidence and our skills, so that we were on sure footing. But the real learning began with the regular season. Then we started putting the strategies we'd learned to the test in the real world. And every step of the way, every game we played, Lombardi and Landry both made sure that we weren't just winning or losing—we were learning from our successes and failures.

When the regular season began, we moved into the Concourse Plaza Hotel, in the Bronx near Yankee Stadium, and our wives came to join us. Life in the Concourse was entirely different from the lifestyles players enjoy today. Even though we all lived in the same hotel, there was very little social life. Our wives gravitated together, because they were all going through the same thing: having a husband who was a football player. Occasionally they'd organize a game of bridge or a small dinner, but otherwise the Giants didn't have any planned social activities. A couple of restaurant owners near the Concourse were glad to see us come in and treated us well, but there were no events that we were obligated to show up to as players have today. There was nothing except what we organized ourselves. We didn't have any of the United Way things or team banquets, no glamour. Instead, we would go out for beers after practice on our way back up the hill from Yankee Stadium. The height of our excitement was stopping at one of our regular places and playing some barroom shuffleboard.

Most of today's players live year-round in the city they play for. They own houses there, instead of living in a team hotel. But in my day, almost no one stayed in New York after the season ended; we all went our own way and had other jobs. Sam Huff went back to West Virginia, Don Chandler to Oklahoma, Frank Gifford to the West Coast, and so on. But during the regular season, we were all at the Concourse. A modern player would probably consider our living accommodations incredibly spartan. My family and I had one very small bedroom; when my oldest daughter was an infant, she slept in the dresser drawer.

We moved there, though, because that's where everybody else on the team lived, so that was where I looked when we came to the city. I wanted to live with the other players and be part of the team. As I've mentioned before, there has been a total shift in the philosophy of kicking and the way kickers are integrated into and included in a team. Back then, I felt it was incredibly important for me to participate and contribute. Kicking was something extra for me, whereas today, it's the beginning and the end for some players.

There are a lot of players who come over from Europe to kick and don't actually ever learn much about the rest of the game. Kickers have a longevity with teams that can be measured in weeks, meaning someone could be kicking for three different teams in a season. They operate in an extremely high-pressure world, like a pitch hitter in baseball. They have one chance to succeed, and confidence has almost everything to do with that success. If a kicker gets into a hot streak, if he gets a good snap from the center and a good holder, he'll just get better and better and start to believe in himself. I remember that the late, great Arthur Daley, who used to write for the *New York Times*, said to me, "When you first came here, you didn't look like you thought you were going to make it. Now, after you've had this success, you look like the most assured person I've ever seen walking on the field."

Confidence—or the lack of it—is exactly why these kickers kick for three or four different teams now. If they can't handle the pressure, they'll find out pretty quickly. But if they're confident and exude that confidence, the team starts to believe in them and they start to play accordingly. I know when I was in a down streak, I used to pray for the Giants to make a first down so I didn't have to kick. As my first season with them progressed, there started to be occasions when I would say to myself, "I hope they don't make it so it comes down to me." Sometimes you just don't want the ball—and sometimes you do. That's when you know you've made it.

Feeling like I was a Giant, like I had made it, meant a lot to me. The guy I replaced, Agajanian, somehow didn't care about that sense of reliance the team members had on each other. He only wanted to come in on weekends and kick, and that's why the team was happy when I came along. They felt it was vital for me to be a part of the team. Nowadays, with the advent of the Gogolaks and the soccer-style kickers who came after, that mentality is gone. Kickers are like their own unit, apart from the team, playing a separate game.

Even though I was firmly a part of the team, and I knew they needed me, I knew I was never going to be a captain or anything like that. I didn't have a regular position. I had four backup positions, and I knew I'd never become a regular in any of those positions because I was too valuable as a kicker. Don Chandler, who was a punter, was in the same situation. He was also a backup fullback, but he had a bad shoulder that wouldn't take the daily pounding. He knew it, and we knew it, and most importantly, Lombardi and Landry knew it. He was part of the team; he ran plays, knew the offense, knew the defense, but wasn't going to be a regular player . . . and neither was I. I occasionally had thoughts and hopes, but there was a part of me that understood, "They're holding me out because they can't afford to get me hurt." A lot of teams operated the same way with their kickers. The Packers of that era, when they were successful, would take Paul Hornung out on third downs so he could rest for his extra-point or field-goal kicking.

At Yankee Stadium, I had Mickey Mantle's locker. It was just coincidence that I got it, no major significance; the Giants just assigned lockers numerically. The closest to the locker room front door were low numbers, and farther out from the front door was where I was, and I was number 88. But even if it was just a fluke, being in the Yankee Stadium locker room and putting my belongings in Mickey Mantle's old locker really made me feel as if I had found my place in life. Having been a visitor in Yankee Stadium as a Chicago Cardinal, I knew how nice the facilities were. But I discovered as a Giant that the home team's locker room was even nicer than the visitors' locker room—and to me, that was saying *a lot*. It was so nice, in fact, that it was unbelievable. We had a clean T-shirt, socks, and jock bundled in front of our lockers every day. The food was better, the accommodations were better, the training room was better, the showers were better. It was just a better situation than anywhere else in the NFL, and every day it felt like walking into a second home.

I never had to worry about cliques, either, as I had on the Cardinals, because I was playing for both the defensive and offensive units. The different units dressed together to some extent, but there wasn't a part of the locker room that I didn't want to go into. People had their sets of friends, of course. The defensive unit, such as it was, sort of stayed together and protected one another, and the offensive unit was the same way. People tended to socialize with their units, and whatever parties they went to on Sunday nights after the games, they'd tend to find guys there from their unit and hang out with them. Each unit lived together, visited together, and went to the same meetings, but for me, I was playing backup positions on both offense and defense, so as time permitted, I went to both meetings. In that respect, I developed a diverse group of friends. Most of my buddies were offensive guys, although I counted many defensive players as close friends as well.

The first regular-season game of 1958 was against the Cardinals. I opened my Giants career kicking against my old team. That's when I first began to understand how important it was to me to feel like a part of the organization. I know it affected my performance. And I also know I was lighter and in better shape than I had been during my days with the Cardinals—and they knew it.

There was a recognizable form to every game I played with the Giants. Jim Lee Howell stood in front of the bench at all times during every game, walking up and down the sidelines. When the offensive unit came off, they would have meetings with Lombardi and he would go through the technicalities of what was working and what wasn't working, along with what he thought would be the next move. Landry, of course, operated the same way with the defensive unit.

The Giants came up with a way to analyze the opposing team during games that was entirely of their invention, as far as I know. Wellington Mara, who owned the Giants, and one of the assistant coaches would be up in the press box with a Polaroid camera, and if we were on offense, let's say, they would take a picture of how the defense of the opposing team would line up against our formations. They would then put that in a sock with a rock in it and throw it out of the press box onto the sidelines, where the Giants had somebody assigned to pick it up. Lombardi would look at the pictures and show them to the quarterback and the rest of the offensive unit so they understood where the defense was lining up, and that's how we'd formulate an attack. That was the beginning of that kind of analysis; now all the teams do it, but with computers instead of socks.

The Cardinals never did anything like that when I played for them. The Giants were simply more sophisticated than any other kind of football playing I'd ever experienced. Sometimes they took a picture just for when the ball was snapped to the defense. And Landry would do the same thing with his defensive unit, having them look at what the offense was doing on those Polaroids. The defensive unit, however, basically stayed in the three different forms of the 4–3 defense, which Landry had perfected.

Landry was an absolute innovator for his time. Steve Owen, another innovator and Hall of Famer, had been the head coach of the Giants for many years, from 1930 to 1953, before Landry arrived. He had created the 6–1 defense, which later became the "umbrella" defense. Landry started with that same idea and, using the same number of personnel, refined it into the 4–3 defense, which is so widely used today that you think of it as a given, a truly basic formation. Landry was the first to put it in place. In fact, I'd go so far as to say that Landry's 4–3 defense has a lot to do with the fame of then Giants linebacker Sam Huff. He was certainly a brilliant player and earned his place in the Hall of Fame, but it's Landry's defensive strategy that made him untouchable. Basically, Landry fixed it so no one could get to Huff.

The 4–3 inside meant that the two defensive tackles and the two ends would take an inside move against their offensive blockers, to contain the inside and keep everyone, except for the center, away from Huff. Nobody could get at him with a blocking angle. That was the defense's first responsibility: to keep the offensive linemen from getting to the middle linebacker. Their job wasn't to make the tackle themselves, but to get in position on the offensive man so Huff could make most of the tackles, which he did.

Landry also instituted the famous flex defense. The flex defense was basically the 4–3 outside, where a tackle occupied the offensive guard. We'd play his outside shoulder, so if the two guards made the initial moves, which we would assume they would, they couldn't get to the middle linebacker. We didn't play that very often, though, because Huff wasn't big enough or strong enough to take on the force of the two guards and the center. If in the first series of downs we saw that the opponent had devised a blocking scheme that would get somebody such as a fullback to block man-to-man on the middle linebacker, Landry would change the defense back to the inside. The blocking of the fullback evolved over the years—he was really the only man who could get to the middle linebacker.

Needless to say, there had been nothing like this with the Cardinals. Sure, there was coaching, but there wasn't much of it. I remember our chain of command for game day. The coach in the press box would call down to the sideline, where another assistant coach would answer the phone and say something like, "You've got to rush the passer." No technique, no tips, no "here's what you have to do to get to the passer," just "You've got to put some heat on the passer. He's killing us." This was a coach talking, and he would say something that any fan could say. That's not coaching to me or to the individual player who's getting those vague comments. If a coach is telling a player to rush the passer, he wants to know how he can become more effective so he can accomplish that. That's what a coach is for, isn't he?

When I was with the Cardinals and I got instructions like that, I had to formulate a method for achieving the objective in my own mind and execute it—again, on my own. Landry and Lombardi, on the other hand, never stopped teaching. They were always communicating in "footballese," so to speak, which was inspiring and helpful. If players weren't doing their jobs, they obviously needed some sort of insight, and Landry and Lombardi would give it to them, albeit in different ways.

On game days, Lombardi would get pretty excited about individual performance. He would holler at people and carry on. Landry, on the other hand, had the same calm demeanor he always had. He would analyze plays cool-headedly, telling us what we had to do in a matter-of-fact way, saying, "You have to execute it *like this*." He would never raise his voice or yell at anybody. All the same, there was no mistaking if he was displeased. We'd know if we had screwed up by his mannerisms. He had a way of looking at us with disgust that pierced to our cores, and we knew, without a doubt, what he meant. That's when I'd understand, almost chillingly, that he might have been calm on the outside, but he was seething on the inside.

I don't think any other coaches in the league matched the caliber of Landry and Lombardi's teaching, but I assume that there were other teams—minus the Cardinals, of course—that had some way of communicating how to do things, rather than just telling players to do them. Paul Brown of the Cleveland Browns, for example, was famous for outsmarting people and being a coach who paid great attention to detail. I still don't know, though, that anybody was as effective as Landry and Lombardi were. They were a big change from the Cardinals' coaches. Because of their teaching ability and the way they handled themselves, we respected their opinions so much more. And it was gratifying for them to tell me how to do something in the midst of a game; then I'd try it and have it work. Although they were two very different men with very different styles, they were both essentially doing the same thing. They were both teaching and doing it incredibly skillfully and effectively. If they told us how to do something and we tried it (and we were physically capable of executing it), it almost invariably worked.

Before games, the offense would sit down with Lombardi, and he would go over his speech and tell us what we had to do to improve and win. Landry would do the same with the defense, while those of us who played both ways went back and forth between meetings, and then Howell would gather everyone for a full team meeting and make a general speech. Players would talk about the difference between Lombardi and Landry and their speeches. The consensus was that both were very good, but also very dissimilar.

Landry was inspiring in his own way. He instilled confidence in us and a belief in what he was talking about. So did Lombardi, but in a style that was a little bit louder and a little bit more colorful than Landry's. Lombardi also had more warmth than Landry, although it didn't make him any more favored by players than Landry.

I know I never heard Landry chew anyone out, whereas I heard Lombardi chew out players often. He never picked on me that I can remember, but he would often criticize a favorite player to make an example. When he was with the Packers, he would yell at Hornung. But Hornung knew that he was Lombardi's "golden boy." When he was coaching the Giants, his "golden boy" was Frank Gifford—so Frank Gifford got the brunt of the tongue-lashings.

Howell was good at picking on Gifford, too. I remember Frank was late to a meeting one time, because he was doing a commercial. "If we're so wrapped up in Madison Avenue and Hollywood that we can't show up for the team meetings, we'd better get out of the business," Howell said. Howell was strict and basically the timekeeper and administrator of the team. He would blow the whistle for practice to start and to end, he would tell us what time the bus left for the airport, and so on. And when he said, "Move," we moved. At the same time, he had the ability, which I think is an unrecognized strength, to delegate authority.

I saw it in a lot of cases. He knew how to recognize talent and work with it. He let Landry and Lombardi do their jobs.

The typical picture of a modern NFL coach is someone who has twenty assistants yet still micromanages everything. Howell was the total opposite. He was completely unlike head coaches today in that he let the assistants run things. Head coaches now seem to feel the need to be involved in every facet of their teams, and I think media attention demands that kind of management to some extent. Here in Dallas—at this writing, at least—Wade Phillips calls the defensive signals, and I think he's regarded less as a head coach and more as a defensive coordinator. Bill Parcells is the example I know best, since I know him best. He has a finger on everything and has everyone reporting to him so he can manage the whole lot, from shoe and T-shirt sizes to weights. Then you have coaches such as Joe Gibbs, sleeping in the office, or Bill Belichick, for whom no detail is too small. They control all the information and all the communication with the news media. Their involvement is totally different from what Howell's was. He made no bones about it: he told the media that Landry ran the defense, Lombardi ran the offense, and he made sure everyone got on the bus and that the meals were served on time. He had a level of humility that would be unthinkable in today's NFL.

There is no way that there would be a head coach who would defer that greatly to his assistants today. No owner would hire a coach who would do that, for one thing. The head coach is the face of the franchise nowadays. But as much as Howell wouldn't fit in today's NFL, I think he was unusual for our day as well. He was unusual, though, because nobody else had Lombardi and Landry. They *couldn't* rely on their assistants the way Howell relied on his—not if they wanted to win. Paul Brown had a reputation for developing head coaches, such as Blanton Collier and Weeb Ewbank, and his assistants had responsibilities with the Browns.

They were the offensive or defensive coach or the offensive or defensive coordinator, but they didn't have the authority that Lombardi or Landry had. Howell deserves much more credit that he gets for giving that authority and for stepping aside and letting them get the glory. As I said, he even told the media that Lombardi and Landry were running the show.

He was still very involved with the team, obviously, and with administrative duties, which he took very seriously. Among other things, he would pass out keys in the hotel and assigned who roomed with whom on the road. In fact, there was a funny incident involving rooming that brought out just how tightly Howell was holding the reins of the operation. He was from Arkansas and thought that anybody from west of the Mississippi, particularly California, had a pretty good chance of being gay. Early on in training camp, Frank Gifford and Harland Svare were roommates. Gifford was from California and the star of the team, and Svare was from the state of Washington. Well, they both had bad backs, as a result of some of the workouts, and they also both slept in the nude.

Our curfew during camp was eleven o'clock, and one of Howell's duties was to check the rooms and make sure everyone's lights were out by then. He always used to check the rooms wearing long blue pajamas and carrying a stopwatch. When he was near Gifford and Svare's room one night, he noticed that their light was on inside and got ready to yell at them. He walked in on them popping each other's backs by standing behind the other guy, grabbing him around the chest, and cracking his back muscles to loosen them up. Gifford was up in the air with Svare standing behind him with his arms around him, they were both in the nude, and the light was on after eleven. Howell came in, looked at the scene in front of him, said, "Oh my God," walked out, and shut the door. I don't recall if the two of them ever roomed together again. He called them into his office the next day and chewed them out for having a light on after curfew, but he didn't fine either of them for it.

I know Howell was concerned about homosexual tendencies. At team meetings, he would say that you have to conduct yourself like a Giant, which I'm sure meant that you were not gay. It also meant that you should be properly dressed for road trips. He would say to us, "Don't wear the gray T-shirts you wear to practice, because it is not part of the contract that we have to dress you." We were told how to conduct ourselves in public and how to speak to the media as well. He insisted that we be careful about what we said about a teammate, what the team was going to do, and our opinions about individual performances in front of reporters.

I'm not sure what the media made of Howell's deference to his assistants or his willingness to occupy himself with administrative tasks and take a backseat, but none of them ever printed anything biting about him. As I said earlier, the media coverage was different because they were friends of ours, and also the reporters were afraid of Howell. They were much more congenial with Lombardi and Landry, surprisingly enough. If Howell saw us talking to the media during a break in practice, he would holler, "Get the hell away from the players!" It was something that got him really riled up.

Another of his duties was to allocate practice time. I never got a sense that Lombardi or Landry were jealous of each other's successes or had any kind of rivalry, except when it came to practice time. Each of them tried to petition Howell for more practice time to work on something, particularly if they had a new series of plays or formations. They had to compete for field time and would give excuses such as "We have the Browns this week!" to try to get more practice time.

The player limit then made a big, big difference with practice. The guys who ran the defensive plays in practice to give the offense a "good picture," and vice versa, had to be the regular players at that time, because we simply didn't have anybody else. Now teams have practice team players and backup players who can play that defensive role. Our regular defensive guys had to illustrate defenses to the offensive unit and be dummies during offensive practice, just as the offensive guys would have to be dummies during defensive practice. Because of that, more fights tended to break out in practice than at any other time, which still happens today. A player will get mad and say, "Why are you hitting me so hard?" and a fight will break out.

The defensive unit always had to give the offensive unit a good picture of what they should expect to see on the following Sunday, and that sometimes led to short tempers as well. Sometimes the offensive players felt that the defensive players weren't giving them a good picture because they wanted the time to relax or work on something else. Lombardi and Landry insisted on getting their pictures, though. They wanted to get the most they could out of every second of practice time. I think they took losses hard, but they always took an analytical viewpoint of both wins and losses and talked them out with us in practices. They had to; there was simply less time to go over things on game days. During game time they dealt with the overall concept and less with individuals. If someone made a mistake, it wasn't as if they could stop the game and say, "Let's run it again." When we won, it was because we did what they said. When we lost, it was because we didn't.

Although both Lombardi and Landry had the same standards and abilities as teachers, I think they respected each other more than they liked each other. Their temperaments were unalike, but they were also dissimilar socially. Lombardi was Catholic, and Landry was Protestant. It was never an issue for them or for us, but there was a time when I thought that if it came down to two players of equal ability, and one was Catholic and one was Protestant, the Catholic one would have been kept, because Wellington Mara was such a devout Catholic. That was my own thought, though, and not one I ever saw come to pass. The ways the owners and coaches made decisions were never revealed to us. We didn't have leaks about one coach sniping at another coach. Now guys tweet between plays, complaining that the coach didn't give them enough playing time or what have you.

Although Howell delegated authority, he was not passive. He was the boss, and he didn't need to do anything to demonstrate his leadership. He had a commanding presence and was a big guy who always carried his stopwatch. With him, Lombardi, and Landry to answer to, I don't imagine any Giant I ever played with would have dared to tweet in complaint.

The media make people want to differentiate themselves from the pack. Privacy has no meaning. We had so much respect for our teammates and coaches, but today's players have a different feeling about what can be divulged, what can be said, and what should be said. They often have no sense of violation, nor do they have respect for and loyalty to their teammates. There would be no place for a guy like Terrell Owens in the past; a player like that wouldn't have lasted with his teammates.

The NFL today has lost of lot of the moral core it had decades ago. We didn't have free agency, the option to go somewhere else, or the Players' Association to fall back on. We had nobody filing grievances, like the five players did against Cleveland Browns coach Eric Mangini during the 2009 season. We thought too much of our job, our teammates, and our own self-respect, and I'm afraid the shift in those feelings mirrors a shift in society in general. The era in which I played was marked by a sense of privacy, dignity, and loyalty. We didn't get into a coach's business, and nothing was filtered out of the office. That sense of loyalty made it a better world. We had an obligation to our teammates and to our fellow man; I think the word is respect.

We lived by the saying I mentioned before: "Once a Giant, always a Giant." It's something you don't really hear said for other teams like you do for the Giants. I feel a connection to current Giants that other former players for other teams might not feel for their old team's present roster, and I know those current Giants also feel a connection to me. This never created a conflict with my broadcasting, although when I first started out, I would say "we" when I was talking about the Giants, saying, "We have to do this" and "We should look out for that." The people at CBS certainly lectured me early on about the use of that terminology, reminding me sternly, "It's not 'we' anymore." It was a hard step to go from "we" to "they," but my connection to and respect for the Giants meant I always was a part of that organization.

I almost forgot. The Giants beat the Cardinals 37–7 in that 1958 game, but it wasn't as close as the score indicated.

CHAPTER 6

The Boss Keeps Time

Now that the 1958 season was in full swing, I started to get more and more of a sense of the different players, the different styles. It was like being part of a big extended family . . . but where all the members were huge, imposing men. We had our stars and our black sheep, and pretty soon we started to develop running gags and favorite stories. And no one was immune—not even Lombardi and Landry. They were Giants, literally and figuratively, but they were also human beings. Knowing that didn't diminish the respect we had for them; if anything, it increased it. They held their position of authority among men who were at times nothing more than overgrown boys.

Most people know Don Maynard from his time on the New York Jets. Not everybody remembers that he was a Giant beforehand. Maynard had a deceptive stride; he didn't give the appearance that he was working hard at any phase of the game. The coaches got down on him for it. In fact, I'll never forget what happened to him in a game against Cleveland, when he was returning punts for us. He fumbled a punt, and Cleveland recovered, and then, not too long afterward, the exact same thing happened again, giving Cleveland a chance to stay alive. When he got back to the sidelines, I happened to be standing close by, and I heard Lombardi say to Jim Lee Howell, "Don't ever let that son of a bitch in the game with a Giant uniform again. Get him out of here." They cut him the next day.

Disciplinary matters were Howell's domain. Among his other administrative duties, he was in charge of cutting players and fining them. He would decide the fines, what times the buses left, and when meetings would commence. He didn't receive input from Lombardi or Landry on those issues that I was aware of. I'm sure as a coaching staff, they discussed fines and penalties, but Howell would most likely tell them what he was going to do and they would concur. There were numerous fines for not making curfew. He didn't check regularly, but when he did, we were in bad shape if he didn't find us in our rooms, in bed with the lights out. Usually, though, the curfew was hardly an imposition. I was always grateful to fall into bed; we worked so hard, and I was always tired. All the same, fines for breaking curfew were among the tamer fines Howell gave.

One of my favorite stories of Howell's disciplining happened when we went to Dallas to play the Colts in a preseason game, the year after I first started playing for the Giants. We loved going to Dallas, although back then, the black players couldn't stay with us in our hotel. It was 1959. During one of the team meetings, Rosey Brown held up his hand and asked where the Mau Maus of Kenya were going to stay when they were in Dallas. Segregation was a tough fact of life in Dallas at that time, but besides Rosey's question, I don't remember anybody seeming to object to the black players staying in a different hotel. It was just a given and nobody asked questions.

What was memorable about our stay in Dallas was not the Mau Maus, but the antics of our linebacker Cliff Livingston. The Colts beat us in a night game, and we were getting ready to go home the next day. We got to Love Field, which is an airport in Dallas, and realized we were missing one player: Cliff Livingston. I had been to a party at an apartment complex the night before with him. At the party, he had, among other things, jumped off the roof of the complex into the swimming pool. I remember nobody thought he would actually do it, even though he was known as being a little wild. When my teammates and I had last seen him at that party, he was with a female companion, and they had gone their own way. So we all assumed he was a goner and loaded onto the plane, ready to leave without him, when Benedict Dudley, the chaplain who traveled with us, said, "Here he comes."

Cliff came through the gates of Love Field with leopard-print Jockey shorts on, and that was it. They held the plane, and I can still see him as he came through the glass doors in his underwear and boarded the plane. Jim Lee Howell fined him $500, which was a big part of your salary back then, but all he said was a curt, "We have to get to the planes on time."

The next week, we played the Eagles in Hershey, and when we were waiting for the plane to go back to New York, Cliff was missing again. Again, we counted him for lost. The plane was at the end of the runway, ready to gun it for takeoff, when all of a sudden we saw a cab come whizzing out of the terminal area, down the runway, and toward the plane. It was Cliff. This time he'd managed to get his clothes on, but since he was late, they fined him again. That time around, Howell called a meeting and gave us all a big talk about how we have to be on the plane on time and how much of a distraction it was if everybody had to wait for one late person. Cliff was fined another $500, so he ended up playing for $1,000 less that season than he had negotiated.

Cliff was a heck of a player, but he was crazy. He came back a different person every year. I think that the year he was fined he was the world's greatest lover. One year, he'd be the world's greatest marksman, then he'd go through another character change and be the world's greatest race car driver the next year. He went through phases, but he was a great player. Nobody hustled like he did. I remember once he stopped an attempt at a punt so well that the player didn't even kick the ball but ran it, and Cliff circled back through the end zone and ran the guy down—that's how much hustle he had. I think that bought him a little bit of tolerance from the coaches, because they usually were fed up with his erratic behavior. When he showed an uncanny degree of hustle, Landry would stop the film during the film meetings and say, "Look at that again."

When we reviewed films, we always watched as a defensive unit and an offensive unit. Lombardi and Landry broke the plays down so that the defense never really had to watch what the offense was doing and the offense never really watched what the defense was doing. We critiqued ourselves, and that was it. That meant that film-viewing was intense. There was never a moment when we could look away and relax, because our individual performances were constantly at risk of being singled out and criticized.

Once, Lombardi was chewing out a player who had a bad game. Lombardi was jumping all over him, and finally the player had had enough. He was a tough guy, and to everybody's astonishment he said audibly, "Vinny, go fuck youself." Lombardi turned the projector off, turned the lights on, and said, "I'll meet you at home plate in Yankee Stadium in a half hour. Nobody talks to me like that."

Everybody was concerned about that prospective meeting, and we went to the player and talked him out of it. We knew if he did anything to Lombardi, he would have been gone. Lombardi was on home plate waiting for him half an hour later, but the meeting never took place. That's the only time I ever remember anyone challenging Lombardi or any of the coaches. We were all alarmed by it. First, we were shocked that the player had said something like that at all, and second, we were shocked that Lombardi had taken it to the next level and the player had agreed to show up—until we talked him down.

That incident didn't end up derailing that player's career in the long term. He went on to have a great football career, but it was actually his mistake in our championship game against Cleveland that led to my making the winning field goal. He's said to me many times since then, "If I hadn't made that mistake, nobody would ever have heard of you." And that's probably true!

Players challenging coaches or each other like that never happened when I was with the Cardinals. There were some guys we didn't like, but we kept those conversations private and away from the practice fields and meeting rooms. Oftentimes we would talk while we were having a beer. We would say how much we disliked one of the coaches or how he didn't know what he was doing, things like that, but those kinds of conversations never left the bar. That incident during the Giants' film meeting was the only time a player got anywhere near a physical altercation with one of the coaches. The coaches would beat us down verbally sometimes, but that was the extent of it.

Come to think of it, there was one time when Lombardi got an accidental beating from a player, but it was in an entirely different context. When I first got to training camp, the colleges all ran the belly series, which was a play in which the quarterback would take a couple of steps toward the fullback, put the ball in the fullback's belly, leave it there for a couple of steps, and then, depending on how the defense reacted, would either leave it with the fullback or take it out and pitch it to one of the halfbacks coming up behind. That play was born from the split T, I think, and they ran it where Lombardi came from. He tried to incorporate it into our offense.

The danger of running the belly series was that the quarterback would get hit a lot, and no team can afford to get its quarterback hurt in the pros. The quarterbacks didn't want to run the play and, as a result, were kind of shabby when we did run it. Finally Lombardi got fed up and said, "Let me show you how to run it as the quarterback." We had a fullback named Mel Triplett who was a good player, a very good blocker, and particularly good at pass protection. He wasn't the smartest guy in the world, though, so when Lombardi got into the drill as the quarterback and told Mel what to do, Mel didn't quite get it.

Lombardi took the ball from the center and started to put it in Mel's stomach and show him how the option would work. Mel didn't understand the concept of the play, and he ran over Lombardi. He stomped all over him, and Lombardi got cleat marks on his neck and chest. Everyone was concerned that he might be really hurt, but he got up and hollered, "That's not how you run it!" He never stopped teaching, but that was the last time we ever ran the belly series.

Besides odd things like that, however, there really weren't too many discipline problems or issues between players and coaches. Lombardi and Landry both put the fear of God in us to act appropriately, especially when it came to being at meetings on time. Lombardi operated on what we called "Lombardi time," which meant that if a meeting was scheduled for eight o'clock, we had better be there at a quarter to eight, ready to go, because he would always start the meetings fifteen minutes early. All he had to do was say "Okay" to start the meetings. He had such a commanding voice; it would get our attention and we'd be ready to listen. He would start the meetings early, and there were no excuses for being late. Since my Giants days, I've lived my life by Lombardi time. When he went to the Packers at Green Bay, they all talked about Lombardi time when we had a game against them. They'd say, "You know what Lombardi time is?" and we'd all nod grimly and answer, "Yeah, we know."

Landry opened his meetings in a much more subtle way. We still had to be on time, obviously, but he didn't have Lombardi's exactness. Nevertheless, when the time came, we knew to be quiet and ready. Lombardi and Landry's attitudes and approach to meetings weren't any different because of our opponent of the week. Their demeanor stayed the same regardless. We would never know who we were playing based on their behavior. They had that consistency.

At the same time, however, Lombardi and Landry didn't necessarily function as a unit; they did their specific jobs apart from each other. They didn't really feed off each other during games. In fact, they rarely spoke to each other, from what I saw. I don't mean to say that they disliked each other. I know they respected each other, but they never really had much conversation. Professionally, they didn't need to talk that much. The only time we ever really heard them interact was when the offense was running against the defense in practice and vice versa. Then they would fuss and yell at each other for not giving a good enough picture of what the other unit could expect.

"Giving a good picture" was a very boring job. To give the offense a picture, we defensive players had to just stand and stand and stand. We were supposed to emulate whatever opponent we had coming up that week. Landry would tell each player specifically, "You're playing Gino Marchetti," for example, "and you've got to do this as an outside, like Marchetti." We'd have to emulate how the guy played as closely as we could. This was something the players giving the "good picture" could be very lackluster about, and Lombardi and Landry would have short words for each other when they thought the other unit wasn't doing it well. And that's pretty much the only times we heard them speak to each other. But both were very effective without the frills; they didn't need to communicate more to make the Giants successful.

Yet, at the start of the 1958 season, we were not as successful as we wanted to be. Early in the season, on October 19, we lost to the Cardinals, 23–6, giving us a 2–2 record at the time (although we went on to end the season with a final record of 9–3). I don't remember our record ever changing Lombardi or Landry's way of teaching or coaching, though. They stuck to the idea that if we did it their way, we would win. If we lost, we weren't doing it their way.

After a win, everybody was happier and there was a lighter atmosphere, but after a loss, the first thing we did was go over films from the previous game. We hated doing that, since we knew that everybody—and I mean *everybody*—would be chewed out for some sort of shortcoming. After a loss, we dreaded going to those film meetings and to practice. We knew whether we had done our job or not, and if I had happened to play well in the game, I would feel more confident; but invariably, even then, they'd manage to find something I'd done wrong. It was amazing how I could leave a game on Sunday, thinking I had done well and wouldn't be criticized in the following meeting or evaluated severely, and then when the time came, they could always find *something*.

I eventually got to know that they wouldn't miss anything. They went over those films with a fine-tooth comb and would call the team's attention to every mistake. Sometimes the other players would say something to the group if they saw one of us do something well that the coaches didn't call attention to, shouting, "Nice play! Good job!" People would speak out in meetings like that, in the darkness. We had to—to keep up morale. But we would get down on each other, too. We could evaluate the films as well as the coaches and see who was doing well and who wasn't. Sometimes Lombardi or Landry would admonish us for speaking up, but not often—they wanted us to learn.

In my view, while they were assistant coaches for the Giants, neither of them was aware of his reputation with us or with the media. I think they knew that what they were teaching was working, based on our results. Nevertheless, when we were 2–2, it didn't make any difference in the way they taught. Nowadays, a coach with a 2–2 record would feel that his career was in jeopardy. Scrutiny is much more intense. Everyone has an opinion or an evaluation, which is one of the reasons why I think the Giants trained so far out, in remote Salem, Oregon. The newspapers didn't have anyone out there who could report on us.

When we did talk to the media, no matter how sore we were over a critique, we always said Lombardi and Landry were doing a terrific job, and we meant it. But Lombardi and Landry themselves never palled around with writers or went to writers to censure players. The writers just knew the amount of respect we had for them. Our comments about their abilities were genuine; no one was trying to curry favor.

Most assistant coaches today are careful about what they say to the press about individual players and head coaches, and most head coaches are not willing to give their assistants or coordinators the authority to even speak to the media, let alone run the entire defense and offense, as Howell did. I think Howell was confident in himself and secure in his position with the Mara family. He knew how loyal they were, so when he saw the abilities of Lombardi and Landry, he let them coach, which, I think, is the most striking thing about Howell.

It's a gamble to let assistant coaches take the limelight. The media relish showing the world an assistant coach's head coach qualities. That's the way Jon Gruden got to be a head coach. He played his hand perfectly. He was a great coach, but in addition to that, he knew how to position himself and market himself, which, I think, is largely due to the head coaches he had. They could have restricted his access to the media, but instead they let him talk and display his head coaching qualities. He was extraordinarily dedicated, and the media got the word out about it, even when he was an assistant. I know that when Gruden was in Philadelphia, if Dick Vermeil slept in the office, then Gruden slept in the office, too, and people got to be aware of that.

Another example is John Fox of the Carolina Panthers. If the head coach of the Giants hadn't let him talk to the media, no one would ever have heard the name John Fox. He and Gruden were able to move up because of their contact with the media. The media found out and publicized what kind of personalities and enthusiasm they had. So it can be dangerous for a head coach to let his assistants get too chummy with the press.

In fact, I remember when I was coaching at Florida State, Tom Nugent said, "Show me an assistant whom the players like and who has acceptance among them and that's the first guy I'm going to fire, because that guy's after my job." A lot of head coaches have that feeling, and with twenty assistant coaches on a team, every man has to be for himself.

But obviously that's not the way the Giants operated. Lombardi and Landry, under Howell's astute direction, had the freedom they needed to make sure we operated as a team, without anybody, whether a player or a staff member, having to look over their shoulders. That meant that they could teach at their optimum level—and we could perform at our optimum level. At the beginning of the '58 season, the gears ground a little as new players like me adjusted to the new circumstances and started to learn the language of Landry and Lombardi. But soon enough, it sank in . . . and we took off.

CHAPTER 7

They Can Get Somebody in Here Who Wants to Play

Back in 1958, the fans weren't used to us winning every week, and neither were we. I think that season got a lot of people wondering *why* we were winning, since we didn't have superior players or the reputation we came to have later on. We did have better coaches and facilities than other teams—Yankee Stadium was *the* place to play—but still, that satisfaction of winning every week felt foreign and tentative. And other teams, such as Cleveland, were winning, too, so we didn't know yet how close we were to coming out on top.

We had started the 1958 regular season by defeating the Cardinals decisively. But after we lost to them unexpectedly, giving us a 2–2 record early in the season, it was time to double-clutch it. We had lost to them at home, 23–6, but didn't see it coming. The Cardinals had a new coach, Pop Ivy, who ran some offensive formations we hadn't seen in a while, and they just gave it to us. But we went on a winning streak from October 26 to November 9, beating the Steelers, Browns, and Colts, which I think was a direct result of Lombardi's and Landry's actions after our surprise loss to the Cardinals. Both Landry and Lombardi went back to basics. For the players, it was like going to training camp all over again.

There was probably some complacency before the Cardinals game. I don't remember being conscious of it, but I'm sure it was there. During a winning streak, we'd hear some proud laughter and get some congratulations, particularly from Lombardi, who would say, "Good job," or "You did this well," but then the moment we lost, all of that would turn into "You forgot the fundamentals! You forgot how to block, how to tackle!" And we had to go back to the basics. It was brutal. After a loss like the one against the Cardinals, there were never any pleasantries. Lombardi was always very vocal with his criticisms but, as I said before, you never knew where you stood with Landry. After a loss, practice became totally different, the way the coaches spoke to us became totally different—their whole personalities changed. And I had to take it from both of them, being on both sides of the ball.

Typically, we had Mondays off to rest up, and in the early part of that season—when we weren't doing so well—we welcomed the reprieve. We'd fill the day by going downtown into Manhattan, going to clubs, and seeing Monday-night fights, things like that. Three or four of us went to the fights together at the Sunnyside Gardens Arena in Queens. It was a fun life . . . except when we lost and were dragging ourselves around town with our heads hanging low.

Normally, practices were pretty routine, but what we did in practice was completely altered after a loss. Lombardi and Landry would amp everything up. They wouldn't make us come in on Mondays, but our practices ran longer and were more intense. They had us go back to basic blocking and tackling drills. We wore pads during practice the week after a surprise loss, something we didn't usually do. It was a good thing we did, though, because there was more contact in those drills. The theme of those practices was, "You clearly forgot how to block, tackle, and catch passes, so these are the things we're going to work on." And it was grueling, working on fundamentals. We had lots of personal contact, lots of tackling drills, lots of blocking drills. It was boring, repetitive, and tough—not a lot of fun. Losing was the worst, but practice the following week ran a close second.

Special teams got a special beating. Back then, because of player limitations, the guys on special teams had to do just about everything. The player limit was thirty-three at the beginning of my career, and by that time it had gotten to thirty-five, I think. We didn't have players specifically signed to play on special teams; they were regular players.

My view was that Lombardi and Landry were looking for a rededication of effort by holding those practices and criticizing us the way they did. I know we hadn't actually forgotten the fundamentals, but *they* thought we forgot or at least that we needed a reminder. Their back-to-basics approach served their purpose, though. We didn't want to go through another hell week, so we didn't want to lose again. Of course, we never *wanted* to lose, but the thought of another grueling week was extra motivation. I think we sometimes forgot just how much it took to win, and they were trying to reinvigorate that commitment in our minds.

They never let up. Both coaches were known as motivators, but those practices sure didn't seem inspirational while we were out there. At the time, they just seemed like drudgery and punishment. Maybe they were doing it by design, as some kind of psychological game to get us so mad that we'd take it out on our next opponent. That could very well have been part of their strategy—I wouldn't put it past them. We just didn't want to go through that punishment again, and that was all we needed to know. In the end, it didn't really matter what they were thinking or what their strategy was, as long as we didn't have to have a hell week again. Before our loss to the Cardinals, we had lost to the Eagles in the second game of the season, 27–24. It was a closer loss, but we still had the same hell week we had after our loss against the Cardinals later.

Those hell weeks came as a surprise to me, naive as I was. When I was with the Cardinals, nothing was done differently after a loss. The coaches didn't double up or anything. We were kind of used to losing. Lombardi and Landry responded to losing in a way unlike any other coaches I'd had. It was like losing was a personal insult to them. We could see it in the way they changed practice and their demeanor after a losing game and then before the next one. But they didn't let losing mess with their heads—they never let their emotions make them irrational. They didn't change their overall tactics, just the practices. They knew what they had to do—it was no mystery as far as they were concerned—and we knew what we were going to have to do. Their meetings usually didn't veer from the normal path, either. There were no fiery speeches of "we'll get them next week," just the same analytical breakdown and teaching us what to do.

As far as I've observed in my playing and broadcasting career, winning makes most coaches friendlier with their players. When we won, though, we got a little bit more of a satisfied, "See, I told you" and "See what will happen if you do what I say?" But losing certainly did make them *less* friendly. I never again or before saw their psychological methods practiced by other coaches to that degree, but then again, the coaches I had experience with were not the teachers that Lombardi or Landry were. They were always teaching. They never took credit for a victory or blame for a loss. They didn't go to the media after a win or a loss and say, "I did it"; it was all on us. They told us to do it their way, and it was because of following through with that, according to them, that we either won or lost.

When we lost and had to go through those punishment practices, it was grim all day long. Nobody talked and nobody laughed in the locker rooms, at meal breaks, or at any other time. It reminded me of the atmosphere after the Yankees lost to the Chicago White Sox in 1964 and Phil Linz famously played his harmonica on the bus after the game. I remember that incident because I was doing the Yankee pregame show then. Yogi Berra was the manager, and I knew both him and Linz from doing the pregame show. Linz had taken out his harmonica while they were on the bus, to break the tension after the loss. At least he said that was his reason for taking it out. He was a little bit of a character anyway, sort of a loose cannon. He liked to laugh and play practical jokes, but after that loss, Yogi was not in the mood for any of that business, so he yelled at Linz to quit playing. Linz didn't hear him, though, and asked Mickey Mantle what Yogi had said, and Mantle said, "He said to play it louder."

That incident was what led people to think Yogi had lost control of the team and when I called him, the people who covered the Yankees were giving him a hard time about the lack of discipline on the team and people joking around after a loss. Yogi was always very helpful and cooperative, but I called him after the harmonica incident and he said to me, "You picked a hell of a time to call."

There was nobody playing the harmonica in the Giants' locker room, I can tell you that. The atmosphere was uptight from losing—we felt that our jobs were on the line. The Giants weren't cutting to make payroll, like the Cardinals were, but because they wanted players who could contribute to wins. There were always players available to take your spot and guys looking for jobs. With only twelve teams in the NFL then and thirty-three or thirty-five players per team, jobs were hard to come by. It was easy to replace someone, and the Giants constantly had somebody new coming in to work out with the team.

Roland LaStarza was a heavyweight fighter who almost beat Rocky Marciano in 1953. In fact, he came closer than any other boxer. He was out of boxing by 1958. He only had three fights that year and was working as a butcher, I believe. Somebody found him and suggested that the Giants give him a workout, and they did. They let him try out, I guess, because of his record against Marciano. It certainly wasn't because of his football prowess.

He had no idea what football was about. He didn't know how to run after a pass, or anything. It was a joke. But the Giants were fairly open and they often gave tryouts to people who had no business being there because they knew nothing about football. I mean, LaStarza didn't even know how to get down into a stance. He didn't have any concept of what was going on in the game or on the field. His tryout was in front of all of us, though. He was in the line and dressed up for practice.

LaStarza's tryout was the coaches' way of trying to send a message that nobody was secure. They were sending the message, "We can get somebody in here who wants to play if you guys don't have any desire to play." They would put notices in the paper that said something like, "Anybody who wants to try out to play for the Giants came come try out. All you have to do is pass the physical."

We didn't recognize anybody else who tried out, except for LaStarza. There would be guys coming in every day who somehow had convinced ownership that they should have a chance. There were always guys who thought "I can do that," and at that time, they were giving people like that a chance, especially after we lost to the Cardinals.

I'm sure this, too, was a motivational tactic, sending the message to all of us that we could be replaced and none of us were safe. However, we didn't have anything to fear from LaStarza. He didn't last very long. He was so inept that he didn't even know enough to be embarrassed. That was the impression I got; I didn't get to know him very well. Nobody they brought in ever made any impact that I can remember. Nobody ever came close to matching the skills we had, so in that sense it was a failed motivational tactic, but it sure kept us on our toes.

They say you learn more from losing than from winning, but I'm not so sure that's correct. We were punished by the things we did in practice and the demeanor in meetings, as well as by what was said in the meetings, but I'm not sure we learned more from losing. We were more fearful, and maybe fear can breed learning, but we really just valued winning that much more because we didn't have to go through that back-to-basics training again.

After a win, when waiting for the coaches to break down the game tape, I at first expected that it would be more about sitting back and savoring the great plays we'd made. But sure enough, it was inevitable that even then, while looking at the films, Lombardi and Landry would find something we did to criticize. When I walked off the field after a win, I would think, "They can't find anything to criticize this week," but it was a false assurance. I kicked the field goals, so that was a clear victory or failure from the result, but the things I did on offense or defense were always uncertain territory. Their criticisms were universal; when it came down to the meetings and evaluations, the coaches were able to find problems with everybody who thought they'd had a good game. It was never a good day. Sometimes they would pick out things I thought I had excelled at and say that my technique wasn't good. Something was always wrong, it seemed like. Both of them had an unquenchable appetite for perfection. We were never as good as we could be.

This idea was new for me in terms of coaching, and it helped me get to another level. Sure, I resented them for pushing me that hard, and so did everyone else, but it benefited me in the end. I never reached what they thought was 100 percent, but I was always improving.

I always thought Wade Phillips had a good eye for evaluating performance. He once told me, "We have guys who think they're giving 100 percent, they're not *really giving* 100 percent." And that's the way Lombardi and Landry felt—that perfection was the ultimate goal. Even though we might think we were giving 100 percent, there was always something left in the tank. I see that happening with a lot of players today, and I think that because

I was associated with Lombardi and Landry, I can spot what Phillips is talking about. I know what he means and can identify what he's talking about, whereas most people don't understand it.

It goes beyond football, too. A person can think he's doing his best . . . and then realize that he's not giving his all. He could be half a step faster, a few pounds stronger. For example, I've seen two games recently where defensive backs got penalized for helmet-to-helmet contact. If they were thinking all the time and at their capacity, they wouldn't have done that, because they know it's going to be penalized. That goes for physical efforts, too. A person might discover that if he reacted differently to a certain situation, he would be closer to giving 100 percent than he is now. I think it's very rare that an individual reaches that goal by both physically giving 100 percent effort and thinking at 100 percent. Looking back, there's always something that could have been done better.

Never on a consistent basis did I feel I had given everything and that the tank was empty. I always felt there was something I could have done that I didn't do, whether I was playing a football game or broadcasting a football game. That was the level of self-examination I reached by playing for Lombardi and Landry. And I think they were at that level because of their spiritual quest for perfection—they say that the way to find God is to seek God. You're never going to find Him completely, yet you have to keep seeking.

It was one of the biggest lessons, if not *the* biggest lesson, I ever learned from them: there is always more left in you than you think you have left.

I did not get this feeling from any coaches I had previously. You never forget the teachers who take you to that next level. I sensed in Lombardi and Landry that their desire for perfection was a result of their spiritual devotion. They were engaged in a quest for perfection that can't be reached by mortals, but their religious quest was evidenced through their football teaching and coaching.

They both respected faith with the same tenacity, the same refusal to compromise. Both of them were extremely devout men, though you might hear about it more in connection with Landry because he did so much work for the Fellowship of Christian Athletes. Lombardi, however, was equally committed to God; in fact, he went to Mass every morning. None of the players on the Giants ever cursed or lost their temper; we all simply knew that our coaches were devout men, and that was to be respected and honored. If there were ever a new player on the team who hadn't yet caught on, we'd pull him aside right away and tell him, "Listen, the coaches are religious. Take it easy." And he'd understand quickly enough.

Landry's faith in particular was something that always awed me about him. I could sense it just from being near him. Even in a room full of football players, in a defensive meeting where we were focusing on the game, I could sense the depth of his belief and his commitment to God. It was an awe-inspiring thing, and something that has influenced me to this day. One of the few times I ever saw him smile was out on the golf course many years after he had been my coach. He held a tournament in Dallas to benefit the Fellowship of Christian Athletes, and he stood at one hole and played it with every group that came through. When my group came to that hole, I told him I'd been baptized the Sunday before.

He said to me, "This is one of the happiest days of my life because of what you've told me." And he smiled.

Both Lombardi and Landry had the attitude that they were going to make us as good as we could be. In Landry's case, that was certainly his goal. I think the reason he used to say "There's only one Lilly" was because Lilly was pretty close to perfection as a player. Watching him, I always thought he could do things

I'd never seen anyone do, but there was still always something he could have done a little better.

I would wonder, "What makes these men so effective as teachers? What makes Lombardi so effective? What makes Landry's method so believable? Why do I buy into what they're saying? Why do both of them stimulate me to want to do better, be a better human being?" I always thought about those questions. I often wondered, for instance, how Lombardi could put up a simple football play, make it interesting, and make me sorry when he was through talking.

I don't know that I ever got any answers, but those were the questions I was asking myself. I think it was their enthusiasm and dedication, but I don't know—how could any human beings get such performances out of people who normally wouldn't reach such heights, myself included?

So even to this day, I always ask myself, "Am I leaving anything in the tank? Can I give some more?" I've applied that lesson on the field and in broadcasting. In my case, those questions have always been positive tools. They weren't pointless self-criticisms; they led to me thinking about how to do things better. I would review my broadcasting tapes, thinking, "Why did I say that? I should have said this instead." Every person I know who has worked as a broadcaster has gone back and listened to themselves, looking for areas of improvement. I think everyone in broadcasting doesn't like the way they sound—at least I've heard a lot of people say that. Realistically (and contrary to the popular saying), most people *don't* like the sound of their own voice. So I learned to go back and listen to what I said, and I'd quickly find myself wondering why I said it that way or realizing that an observation I made wasn't that important.

Most of my approach was to watch myself on tape. Sometimes I would watch with John Madden, my broadcasting partner. Madden and I would critique each other, but we never had a cross word. We were always honest with each other, yet respectful—it was one of the secrets to our success. Madden would get down on himself for mistakes in identification, such as saying a team was in a certain defense when they obviously were not. He was very self-critical. He had that happy-go-lucky air about him, but it wasn't necessarily his essential self. I think it was more his television personality.

There were moments when I'd think, "I nailed that," but rarely. Frankly, I always knew that I must have been doing something right, because I wouldn't have gotten the recognition and assignments I did if I weren't doing something that people liked. That sounds egotistical, I suppose, but after the criticism and evaluation, I would think that, at the end of it all, somebody must like it. But even though there were times I thought I did a good job, I would still go back and look for things to work on.

It goes back to the lesson I learned from Lombardi and Landry: There is always something I can improve on. That lesson was their greatest legacy to me.

CHAPTER 8

"Believe in Your Heart That You'll Win"

Lombardi spoke the following words in his famous "number-one speech," which he gave in 1970 and which has been quoted over and over again as one of the most inspirational speeches ever given. They are the words that square best with the Vince Lombardi I knew. He's the man who told me, unequivocally, "You've got to believe in your heart that you'll to win."

Every time a football player goes to ply his trade, he's got to play from the ground up: from the soles of his feet right up to his head. Every inch of him has to play. Some guys play with their heads. That's okay. You've got to be smart to be number one in any business. But more importantly, you've got to play with your heart, with every fiber of your body. If you're lucky enough to find a guy with a lot of head and a lot of heart, he's never going to come off the field second. . . . It is a reality of life that men are competitive and the most competitive games draw the most competitive men. That's why they are there: to compete, to know the rules and objectives when they get in the game. The object is to win fairly, squarely, by the rules—but to win. And in truth, I've never known a man worth his salt who in the long run, deep down in his heart, didn't appreciate the grind, the discipline. There is something in good men that really yearns for discipline and the harsh reality of head-to-head combat.

But he wasn't just talk and bluster. Along with passion, he knew that the grind and discipline were necessary. I remember him saying once, "The human body is a marvelous machine that has never been matched. Once you get it in shape, it can recover from almost anything." I think he would still believe that today, even though players today don't endure the same sort of physical pounding we did.

The beatings we took had a lot to do with the player limit; as I've mentioned throughout this book, we didn't have the luxury of many backups, which meant that we had to play when we were hurt. How fast we were able to come back after being injured, how quickly we healed, and how we played through pain without letting it affect us were almost signs of valor and manhood for us. It was almost like we had to do those things to be a member of the team.

I don't think that mentality exists today, at least not like it did then. The protective equipment is better now—it's lighter, for one thing. It doesn't absorb moisture like it did, which means players are probably as fast in the fourth quarter as they are in the first quarter, because the old equipment would absorb moisture and get heavier and heavier as we perspired through a game. The shoulder pads, for example, got heavier as they got wet. No matter how cold it was, we perspired underneath. Now protective devices are made of materials that won't absorb moisture. The jersey will get heavier, but that's minimal. They even have the technology so that clothing just wicks off perspiration.

Along with better equipment, I think the tolerance for pain has gotten to be a big difference between past and modern football. If a player pulled a hamstring back in my day, it didn't keep him out for a month. He just played through it or they shot it with Novocain or something similar. For instance, I mentioned earlier that I broke my arm during my rookie season. It wasn't set properly, so I actually played my second year with my arm in a metal cast. The cast had to be approved by the referees before each game, but I went out there with my broken arm and played. Today's football players have nothing on toughness compared to the ones in my day. This is probably due in part to the size of their contracts and the advice or their agents, but in that earlier time, nobody had an agent and it was just a mark of being part of the team that we played when we were hurt.

I don't recall players ever going up to Lombardi or Landry and asking not to play because of an injury. I remember guys getting banged up, but they usually just kept it to themselves. They didn't want word to get out to the opposing teams that their left shoulder, say, was hurt, because if the opposition knew where someone was injured, that's where they would attack. We would see people getting taped up in the training room and, as friends, we'd ask where they were hurting, but other than that, it would be pretty much a secret.

The NFL has rules about disclosing injuries today that were not in place then. The reason they were incorporated was so nobody would have knowledge that wasn't general knowledge. That's why they put injuries in the paper and why it has to be done by a certain day of the week. In this way, gamblers won't have any advantage of inside knowledge about who is hurt. The requirement to disclose all injuries changed the game. The opposition can pick up a newspaper and *know* to attack a player from the left side. That definitely alters the game plan.

Of course, even though he insisted on toughness, deliberately gunning for a player's injured spot would be something Lombardi would have considered dirty pool. But he wouldn't have been above it if it meant winning a game. Both he and Landry were models of mental and physical toughness—after all, Triplett ran over Lombardi when he was trying to illustrate the belly series, and Lombardi survived.

It was rare, though, that either of them displayed their own physical toughness. They usually didn't demonstrate techniques. Landry's tackling technique of putting your head behind, for instance, was different from almost anyone else's that I'd been exposed to, but he didn't demonstrate it. He believed that if you tackled somebody in the open field, you should put your head behind his body, instead of in front, like most coaches teach, to eliminate the cutback. He and Lombardi would tell us what they wanted us to do and how we should do it, but it was rare that they would show us how it was done themselves. The techniques were so thoroughly explained by both of them that we rarely had questions to ask.

We all knew these were two smart, strong men from their reputations and from the way they conducted themselves, talked, and presented things. I knew Landry's reputation as a tough football player—I had seen him play and had played against him myself long before I came to the Giants, although back then, I didn't quite hold him in the reverence I later did. But I knew he was a good player.

Lombardi just exuded confidence and toughness in the way he talked and acted. He had been a lineman and was in fact one of the "seven blocks of granite" at Fordham. However, by '58 standards, Lombardi was lighter and smaller than most football players. He was short and stocky, but nevertheless we never got any sense that he wasn't or hadn't been a tough guy.

There were some coaches on the opposite end of Lombardi and Landry, who had never played the game. There were very few of them, but they were there. There also are some coaches in football today who either never played at all or never played in the NFL. Some of the brightest lights in NFL coaching today didn't have brilliant playing careers. Brian Billick, for example, was a tight end who played in college, as Lombardi did, but then got cut by San Francisco. Although his father was a longtime scout for the

Naval Academy, Bill Belichick played only a little bit in college. Jon Gruden, whose father was a coach, was a backup quarterback in college. Bill Parcells never played in the pros; he was a high school coach in the beginning and worked his way up.

I find that most of the gifted athletes, the guys who didn't have to work hard at perfecting their techniques, don't make good coaches. It's the guys who had to work on techniques and slowly make their way up who make the good coaches, such as Ralph Houk, who was a second-string catcher for the Yankees, and Joe Torre, who after winning the 1971 National League MVP continued on as a good player but not great by any means. They both later became amazing managers. Joe Girardi, in the same vein, was largely a platoon catcher before he became a manager. The guys who really had to work on things that didn't come naturally to them become the good coaches. They are the guys who had to learn and who wind up being the ones who pay attention to detail.

Of course, Lombardi and Landry always paid attention to detail. When our record was 2–2 in 1958, they didn't falter in their attitude or game plan. They went over our films, retaught us the fundamentals, and the next thing we knew, we had a three-game winning streak. On October 26 we beat the Steelers (who weren't very good at that time), 17–6, then went to Cleveland to beat the Browns, 21–17, and back home to beat the Colts. We were taking care of business after that grim week of losing to Chicago.

During the Steelers game, Carl Karilivacz had a twenty-three-yard fumble return. I made the extra point and then they made a field goal, we made a field goal, they did again, and we did again. Don Heinrich had a one-yard rush. It was a very work-manlike game. We were supposed to win—and we did. It was sort of routine and not extremely memorable, but after that, things lightened up as much as Lombardi and Landry would allow them to lighten up. They let us take off our pads and get back to wearing sweats during the practices before our game against the Browns, giving us the sense that they were thinking, "Okay, you got the message."

Cleveland was our league competitor at the time. It was always something special to get ready for and play Cleveland. They were always looming large on our minds—we would watch to see what they did in their games, because we knew they had good personnel and that we would usually have to play them twice. So after beating the Steelers, we had a serious week, I can tell you that. You could see a little more intensity in everybody on the Giants. Our players and coaches had such respect for Paul Brown. There was an admiration among the coaches for the way he ran things, which was probably a little extra incentive for them as well as for us. It meant something personally to beat the Browns—they didn't really need to tell us. They did, but we didn't need to hear it.

We didn't always know who the quarterback was going to be; it was either Frank Ryan or Milt Plum, and neither one was highly regarded in our stadium. But the Browns had some good players at every position, and we were aware of that. For example, the first thing that scared us when we looked at the Browns' offense was Jim Brown. We knew we had to adjust our defense and play a little bit differently to combat him, because he was just so good. They had good players at other positions, but we knew he was the one we had to stop to win.

He was another one besides Lilly who was a man among boys. Brown was so talented, so big, and so fast. He was unstoppable. I remember he would get up slowly after being tackled, but he didn't miss a down. Sometimes I would think he was hurt by the way he walked back to the huddle, but the next time he carried the ball, I knew he wasn't hurt. I think that was part of his act.

He also didn't warm up with the rest of the team. He would run around the stadium. The rest of them would be dong calisthenics to warm up and he'd just be trotting around the field. It was almost scary. He was such a physical specimen and such an impressive-looking guy, and he ran around the field while the rest of the guys were doing calisthenics. Why would Paul Brown let him do that? I always marveled at and wondered about those sorts of things—he got into my head. I remember his reaction to the field goal I kicked to beat him in the playoff game—he always said that was one of the most disappointing moments in his career.

I never knew him very well—we were never social pals—but, among other things, I played basketball with him on the *Sports Illustrated* team one year during the off-season. He was amazing on the basketball court, too. He would just flex his arms and guys would come flying away from him. He was a frightening figure, and everyone held him in such respect and awe.

Yet it's been my experience that a lot of people today—even those who are involved in the game at a high level—don't know who he is, which I find unfathomable. I just don't know how that can be. I think that it is most likely that there are people who don't know who Landry or Lombardi are, either, although I don't think there are many people here in Dallas who don't know Landry. The name might not ring terror in their hearts, though.

The idea is astounding to me—not just that these individuals don't know who Brown is, but that Lombardi, who was the face of the NFL for so many years and who has the Super Bowl trophy named after him, isn't known by people involved in the game. That's another of the problems with the game today: people don't know the history.

Modern players and coaches might say, "What do I need to know that for? I just need to know the playbook," but as a player, fan, or coach, you should know it's important information. It's like a golfer knowing that Arnold Palmer is the guy who built the PGA Tour. The reason golfers are making big paychecks on the PGA Tour is because of a guy like Arnold Palmer. That's why they should know about football history: for the same reason they should know who George Washington and Abe Lincoln are.

There are plenty of places outside of Dallas where if you said, "Tom Landry," you'd get the response, "Who?" For somebody who has been as close to the game as I have, it is staggering that people heavily involved in the game today wouldn't know who Jim Brown is, not to mention Landry and Lombardi. We live in an era of unprecedented communication, in which there is an abundance of sports talk stations and information available on television, radio, and the Internet. But it seems that the more information there is, the more the actual history seems to get buried. It's appalling to me, but then again, history and football have always been two of my biggest loves.

And that's why I can so easily get lost in remembering 1958.

When you look at the statistics, we just drubbed Cleveland in our game against them. We had 22 first downs; they had 11. We had 12 complete passes; they had only 4. We had 197 yards in the air; they had 26. We sacked them twice, and they sacked us only once. The total yards were 337–201 in favor of the Giants. I could go on and on.

But if you look at the scoring, it was a really tough game. We had to grind out a come-from-behind victory. Lou Groza kicked a forty-two-yard field goal in the first quarter, we got a touchdown in the second quarter, then Jim Brown scored, and then their Kenny Konz scored on an interception return. When we went to halftime, we were down, 17–7. Then Alex Webster caught two passes—one in the third and one in the fourth to get a touchdown, and we kept scoring for the rest of the game. I remember I missed a field goal, though.

Jim Brown was a personal challenge to our fullback, Mel Triplett. Triplett thought he was just as good as Brown, but he wasn't. However, he always had good days against the Browns. During that game, he had a good day running the ball and particularly with protecting the passer blocking, as I remember. He was an excellent pass protector and did well picking up people who got loose from offensive linemen in that game. Triplett had 116 yards to Brown's 113 yards. Triplett didn't score himself, but he outgained Jim Brown, and that was a *big* accomplishment to him. It satisfied the personal vendetta he had.

When we came into the locker room at the half down 17–7, the Browns appeared to be imposing their will on us. We weren't getting run out of the park by any means. We were behind, but not badly. I don't remember the mood, but it usually was very businesslike in the locker room at halftime. One of the things Brian Billick says in his book *More Than a Game* that struck me was that what with halftime pep talks and appraisals, once everyone goes to the bathroom and gets settled down, halftime is over—and that's about the way it was with us.

We had five minutes, probably, to get with our groups and talk among ourselves about what we had to do, who was having a good game, and who was having a bad game. Then we met with the coaches, either Lombardi or Landry, who told us what to do to get back into the game or to win the game. But during Giants halftimes, there were never any inspirational, ground-shattering announcements that I can recall. They just said either to keep doing what we were doing or to do such-and-such.

Cleveland was undefeated going into that game; their record was 5–0. That added something going into the game. We had to beat an undefeated team to win the game. Nothing changed when we were down, though. Lombardi and Landry still believed we had the right formula and that they had taught us the right things. We just had to execute better and perform better individually.

In boxing, they say everybody's got a plan until they get hit. Well, Lombardi and Landry didn't change their plan even though we'd been hit. I think that's a pretty powerful message. Players watch the coaches to see if they're panicking. I remember my days with the Cardinals, when I would see the way the coaches reacted and think, "If they don't believe, how can we believe?" I'd glance over at the sidelines out of the corner of my eye, to see if they were clenching their fists. I could see Cardinals coach Joe Stydahar's frustration, and I think it transferred to his players. It left a feeling of "I don't know what to do." He was a guy who would get hit and then not have a plan.

The better the coach, the better they are at masking their emotions. If Bill Parcells had been coaching the '58 Giants, I don't think anything would have changed in the locker room. It still would have been very businesslike. In a situation like that, when we were down but not out, they remained completely confident. They never had a defeatist attitude. They made us believe that if we did what they said, we would come back. It was up to us to say when. That is an incredibly significant message that seems so obvious because of who they were and what they did, but that's not how most people are in life.

I hope that their message will influence any coaches who read this book. You have to ask yourself, "How much confidence am I displaying, and how is that affecting the people around me?" Lombardi and Landry were so sure that if we continued to play the defense or offense as they taught it and if we gave a little more effort and corrected the mistakes we made, we would be successful—even if we had Jim Brown jogging around on the field and in our heads and even if we were playing against an undefeated team.

I think there are coaches today who lose it like Stydahar. Everybody tries to talk in a positive way and gives that chipper front, but that's not how they really feel, and it shows. They think the other team is better. Sometimes I would pick up on that attitude in a coach when I was broadcasting. If I sensed that, however, I kept it to myself. It was not part of reporting the action, only something I surmised. I *never* got that impression from Lombardi or Landry.

And there are plenty of instances when coaches go beyond being unable to mask their emotions to actually being ruled by them. Just think about the Raiders incident early in the 2009 season when the head coach broke an assistant's jaw. I think that snapping point isn't just a personal failing, it also comes from the whole organization, who the owners are, and so on. In the case of Raiders' owner Al Davis, a friend of mine whom I like a lot, I think he put such pressure on those coaches that they went berserk. For example, I had a special teams coach tell me that they had a camera follow him during practice to find out what he did when it wasn't special teams practice. I think the whole organization reflects how the coaches react to the pressures, the halftime score, the whole package.

If a coach is unsure of his backing, that shows itself in his game. The Mara family and their loyalty to Lombardi and Landry at that time made it possible for those two coaches to be so confident in what they said at the half and what they did during games or during practices. Even so, every coach is always looking over his shoulder and wondering what ownership is thinking. As John Madden often said, "Winning is a great deodorant."

Coaches also had a little more rope in those days. Now it's much shorter. A coach with an 0–5 record, like the Tennessee Titans' coach Jeff Fisher, might not have the chance to finish out the season like he would back then. The added pressure means a tendency to snap more, which I'm not sure makes for a better game.

People respond positively to confidence in leaders, not agitation or frustration. The fact that Lombardi and Landry never lost confidence under pressure brought out the best in all of us.

CHAPTER 9

Treat Everyone the Same

Once we were back on track and had the confidence of a win against the Browns under our belts, we were virtually unstoppable. In the regular season of '58, we lost only one more game—to the Steelers. To be honest, I don't remember the details of our winning streak, except that we were all on an emotional high. Sunday nights and parties after the games were always upbeat. The coaching staff also had a different approach now that we had gotten some momentum. "Let's keep it rolling. What we're doing and teaching is working" was the message they seemed to send.

They pushed us to avoid complacency, which was not an option to them. There always was a sense of urgency when they were teaching and presenting the game. They always told us that this was a good team we were playing that week, that it was no time to rest on laurels, and that we had to continue playing like we were playing. With all their messages, I don't remember us even getting close to anything like complacency. Lombardi and Landry never let the thought that our opponents weren't worthy enter our heads—that was a crucial part of their method of teaching. After all, even the worst NFL team is still an NFL team. Like us, they would know that they have to do what it takes to win. Furthermore, they would know we were on a winning streak and would want to stop it—and there's no underestimating that as a motivator.

Even today, when the Cowboys play a team like Atlanta, I still think the Cowboys are going to have a tough time. Maybe this is because of my training and indoctrination from back then; they taught me never to take anything for granted, which is an important life lesson.

When I was on the Cardinals, when we were about to play a team that didn't having a winning record, there was the feeling of "misery loves company." We felt a kinship with them, plus a little bit of hope that we finally had a chance to win one, since they were as bad as we were. On the other hand, we were on guard against a good team. It was like playing the Yankees today. Everyone is judged against them and how good they are, and playing against them is a team's chance to be judged favorably.

Playing on a solid team like the Giants, I knew everyone was gunning for us, and I realized that we would always get the opposing team's best effort if they had anything at all left in the tank. Playing us was their one chance to get respect. It was also a chance for individual players to get a better contract or paycheck.

One thing about the Giants' team concept was that I don't ever remember anyone ever thinking about how good his reputation was or how much money he was making. Money never entered our judgment of how good a player was or affected the way anyone approached how he was going to play. I don't remember any resentment about how much money anyone else was making. Of course, there were never the kinds of salaries that are commonplace today. The amounts were smaller back then and so were disparities. Some guys were making $25,000 and everyone was aware that they were highly paid, but that didn't become a factor in how we approached the game or thought about them. I suspect that that same attitude prevails on the good teams today as well, but on the teams that don't have a strong a culture of cohesion, discrepancies in pay become a serious problem, and it shows out on the field.

I know this because I ran into that kind of poisonous thinking on the Cardinals. My contributions were greater than others' on the Cardinals, I thought, and yet they were making more money than I was. I thought about it, and I'm sure others did, too. But I didn't discuss it with my teammates. A guy was getting paid to win, but he wasn't even performing, and that just took the team farther down.

At that time, salaries weren't reported in the papers. It's hard for the modern fan to understand that. One of the great dangers of going to a Pro Bowl in those days was that it was an opportunity to discuss how much we were making with comparable players. The kicker for the Eagles, for example, was someone I talked with about how much he was making. Likewise, the defensive backs would meet their compatriots from other teams and talk about their salaries. The owners always said to us, "Don't discuss your contract with the members of the other teams," but it was inevitable that we would get around to talking about what the disparity was between the payment for a defensive back on a team such as the Eagles, say, and the Giants. It would often come up while we were all in the bars together, waiting for a meeting to get started, or during a quiet moment in practice: "How long have you been playing? What are you getting paid?"

It was sort of an agenda for players heading to the Pro Bowl. It was a chance to get that question answered; in many ways, it was like a union meeting disguised as a Pro Bowl. We talked about our relationships with the ownership and coaches, too. Nobody was coy; everybody wanted the information. But because there was a lot of pride involved, the conversations weren't always easy. Instead, we would get into vicious circles: "How much are you making?" "You tell me first." "No, you tell me first." Certain teams had the reputation of being very stingy, and certain teams had players who flatly refused to talk about money.

When I was still with the Cardinals, I went to a function and George Blanda was there. He was quarterbacking for the Bears, and I asked him something about George Halas. I don't even remember my question, it was something innocuous, but he said, "Mr. Halas told me not to discuss that with opposing team members," and he wouldn't say anything more. He was very correct about what Halas told him to say and not to say. Football players were expected to be company men in that regard. However, we mostly didn't conform to those "company" rules in the Pro Bowls. Things might be embellished a little bit, but we got a lot of information.

We would go back and use that information to justify our own contracts. For example: "Lou Groza plays full time and kicks. I play part time and kick, so I should be making this amount." Players would learn things during the Pro Bowl that they could take back into their negotiations the following year, such as "This guy is making that much more than I am." They'd use information as a negotiating ploy, especially since there were no agents to do that for them.

Negotiating didn't always work out, though. As I'm sure you've heard, one year, Jim Ringo, the all-pro center for the Packers, went into negotiations with Lombardi when he was the Packers' head coach. He brought his agent to the meeting. Lombardi said, "I don't negotiate with agents. Hold on, let me make a phone call." He turned away, picked up the phone, and the moment he hung up he said, "I told you I don't negotiate with agents. You've just been traded to Philadelphia." Ringo was one of his best players and an all-pro for several years, but Lombardi chose to trade him rather than deal with his agent. I think it was sort of an unwritten rule at that time not to bring others into negotiations because nobody had agents or other people speaking for them.

When Landry and Lombardi were assistants in '58, I'm sure they had a pretty good idea how much everybody was making.

As coaches, they had to know what management thought of the individual players. It was their job to know, for example, that Gifford was making more than Byron Bailey, who was a backup running back.

The Giants players, on the other hand, never thought about who was getting how much, and I think that came from the leadership we had in Lombardi and Landry. Money never affected the way they conducted themselves in film evaluations or in meetings; they evaluated our performance in terms of who was playing and who was not; money was never a consideration. Whenever they would chew out people who weren't performing, it was never financially motivated. I know Jimmy Johnson would say to a headliner like Troy Aikman, "Hey, I'm going to chew you out in practice today, but don't take it to heart, because this is what I have to do." He would qualify it before practice or a film session even started and tell the superstars, "I'm going to chew you out today. I have to do it to affect the rest of the team, so they think I'm treating everyone the same." I don't know that Lombardi or Landry ever did that—they actually *did* treat everyone the same. I think it was just part of their natures.

Lombardi and Landry both served in the military. Lombardi came from West Point, where he worked with Red Blaik. Lombardi's first pro job was with the Giants, and he treated us in a very militaristic style, as did Landry. Landry had been in the service as a bomber pilot, so military discipline was thoroughly ingrained in both of them, and I saw it reflected in the way they coached. In a platoon, they don't treat the stockbroker's son any differently from the ditch digger's—everyone is treated like a dog.

Their military influence extended beyond their egalitarian style. As I already mentioned, we operated on Lombardi time, which meant that fifteen minutes early was on time. We had tightly organized practices as well, and abided religiously by Howell's stopwatch. On other teams, if the offensive practice is not going well, the coaches will let their practice go until they get it right, but this was not so in our case. They stuck to the specific times they had agreed on, as they do in the military. There were no variations or exceptions made in weight requirements; you had to weigh in at a certain time and be a certain poundage. They made rules and requirements, and we followed them. Their methods always came back to the philosophy of "If you do it my way, we'll win," and we usually did. I've found that other coaches who don't abide by those codes aren't as rigorous or detailed in their teaching of technique or in the way they present plays, and therefore have less authority over their players . . . and, ultimately, less success on the field.

However, even though they were strict, I don't remember either Lombardi or Landry ever criticizing us if we made a physical mistake. They understood that, or they seemed to. But if we made a mental error, we were in trouble. They made sure we knew it was because we weren't studying enough, didn't understand the assignment, and on and on. If they disciplined a player, that usually meant fines, which were significant because no one was making that much money to begin with. We also had to do extra laps or push-ups after practice.

I was certainly fined or made to run laps a few times, but I accepted it because it meant that I had let the team down. I was never upset with them for disciplining me, but at myself, and I'm sure my teammates felt the same way when they were disciplined. The punishments Lombardi and Landry instituted were deserved most of the time; they weren't given out just to show who was boss.

That's not automatically the case with most coaches. I can testify to that based on my experiences on other teams and what I witnessed as a broadcaster. Superstars, as I've said, are often treated with kid gloves. As a team, we Giants appreciated the fairness of Lombardi and Landry. They may have been task-masters and drill sergeants instead of "players' coaches," but they were fair and consistent. Indeed, one of the things I hear about coaches, officials, and players today is that people wish they were consistent. For instance, a coach might say he doesn't mind when officials make bad calls, as long as they're consistent. Our two coaches were very consistent.

Of course, I know the term "players' coach," but I would like to think that I don't know what it means. To me, a pure players' coach means a weak individual who shows favoritism and has easy practices, in shorts and T-shirts, not pads, and allows a general lack of discipline on his team. In instances when players' coaches win, it is just random good luck. I think the general consensus in the NFL is that it takes a guy who is organized and a disciplinarian to be successful—someone with the reputation of a coach such as Bill Cowher. He was friendly with the players and was a players' coach in that sense, but was a very strict disciplinarian as well. He'd fine the guys who were superstars just like he'd fine the guys who were underlings. Tony Dungy is another coach who was a players' coach in the sense that he was a guy who got close to the players and told them, "My door is always open." Players could go and talk to Tony, but they had better abide by his rules, too.

George Halas might also have been considered somewhat of a players' coach, yet he also won more games than anybody except Don Shula. And I guess you could say that all the guys liked Shula, but he had that hardness, that disciplined core about him that people respected as well as liked. I never played for a players' coach, but I think that when Tom Nugent at Florida State told me he'd fire any assistant who went around courting the players' favor, I think he was warning me against becoming just that: a players' coach.

I don't think that any coach in the NFL should be purely a players' coach. That's not what they're paid to do. Lombardi and Landry were certainly not players' coaches, but they had that balance of openness and discipline. They ran the team as if it were a military unit. I've heard that the new coach in Denver, Josh McDaniels, apparently learned attention to detail from Bill Belichick, whose disciples are all over the league now. However, Belichick learned from Bill Parcells, who learned from Bob Knight, having worked for him as a basketball coach. Knight also was a big Lombardi disciple. Knight's primary influences, based on our conversations, were Lombardi and maybe Red Blaik. That tough outer shell, then, has its roots in the Lombardi and Landry days.

Everybody says the game has changed, but the reality is that you can trace its lineage from Belichick and his disciples up to Parcells up to Bobby Knight up to Lombardi and, behind him, Red Blaik, so when you talk about influence, Lombardi isn't just a name on a trophy. If it hadn't been for the kind of respect and admiration he commanded, his name wouldn't even be on the trophy. His influence is still felt, even by coaches who don't know who he is and think that the trophy is named after a rest stop on the New Jersey Turnpike! The main thing is that when you look at Belichick and the people who coached under him, you can see they are attempting to instill that same sense of discipline that Lombardi and Landry did.

You can see the influence of Lombardi and Landry in other top coaches as well. Jim Caldwell, the head coach of the Indianapolis Colts, patterned his coaching style after Tony Dungy, whose primary influence was Tom Landry. Dungy is religious and low-key, like Landry, and his philosophy boils down to "Do it my way and you'll win." Sound familiar? Caldwell seems to have taken the same approach. In fact, he's somewhat Jim Lee Howell-like in his willingness to delegate responsibility to a trusted assistant. In Caldwell's case, he successfully relies on Tom Moore, his offensive coordinator and quarterback guru, the man whom Payton Manning depends on.

Successful coaching methods have not changed that much, then, and I do not think players have, either. They have more money, but other than that, they haven't changed that much. If players are fundamentally the same, contrary to what the media say, and so is the coaching system, then Lombardi and Landry would still be successful at having players receive their message. The military model still holds in pro football. The most disciplined teams are the most successful ones. The teams where the chain of command, from the owner to the general manager to the head coach to the assistant coaches to the players, is muddied, typically don't meet with success. Football is still a warlike sport, and the preparation for "going into battle" still requires a military sense of discipline.

You keep hearing about the "modern player," whether it's in basketball, football, or any other sport. The modern player is someone who is so into himself, his statistics, and his own outcome that he can't be coached and won't listen. Everybody says that coaches can't use the same kinds of discipline on these players anymore, but they can. It's still about peer pressure. I can see this because I'm closer to the game than most people. There's nothing like peer pressure, just as there's nothing like acceptance from your teammates. There's no pride like the pride earned from doing a job well in front of one's teammates. And there is no disappointment like letting them down or garnering their disfavor. That hasn't changed at all. More money and different methods of transportation and communication have changed things, but I don't think that, deep down, the character of the NFL players has altered a whole lot. Human nature is human nature. Disciplined teams succeed; those teams with a "strong locker room" can bring out the best in players who might not have had much peer pressure on other teams.

The media have been saying that the NFL has a huge image problem because of players' off-the-field 3:00 A.M. stunts. We read about it, we hear about it, but for the most part, I don't think the NFL has that problem; the attendance figures and television ratings surely don't indicate that. I just don't buy it. I think it's more of an embarrassment than a huge crisis. The media criticism is nothing more than throwing spitballs at a battleship—it's not meaningful. Behavior problems are a blot, no question about it. Pacman Jones is a blot, but players like him are the exception, not the rule.

Take the rehabilitation of Michael Vick. I talked with Tony Dungy, who is his mentor, when he was here in Dallas, and his philosophy was that everyone deserves a second chance. I think very highly of Tony, and if Michael Vick does what Tony says, he'll be okay.

People have overhyped the whole situation of Michael Vick returning to the game. Frankly, I never thought he was that good a quarterback to begin with. He never bought into the idea that he was a drop-back, pocket quarterback (those are the ones who, in the long run, have been successful). He was always looking to run the ball instead of throw it. Even though a pass play might have been called, he would look for a way to physically get out of it. I don't think Atlanta was ever going to be a championship team with Vick as a quarterback, and it doesn't look like there's really a role for him in Philadelphia, but that seems to be more of a football decision than a psychology or fan-based decision.

With cases like a Jones or a Plaxico Burress or a Vick—the more extreme discipline cases—I don't think Lombardi or Landry would have kept them around very long. They might have given them a second chance, but not a long period of tolerance. Steve Howe had seven "second chances" with the Yankees, which would never have happened if he were a football player for the Giants. Howell, Lombardi, and Landry had strict expectations for our off-the-field behavior. There was no dividing line from when it was our private business and when it was the team's business— it was immediately the team's business. As I told you, Howell chewed Gifford out in front of everybody when Gifford was late to practice after shooting a commercial. He told him that he would be gone the next time he showed up late. It's a perfect example of how rigorously they avoided giving anyone special treatment.

Everyone had a responsibility to do his job as a member of the team, which they instilled in us strongly, and therefore there was not really much tolerance on the team for somebody who was hanging around late or showing up to practice unprepared. Additionally, if someone went out and got drunk, he went with a teammate, he didn't go with a group of friends. This wasn't so much a written team rule as an implicit understanding; it was part of the public image we were all conscious of projecting. Today, Tony Romo, for example, has an entourage that goes with him wherever he goes. They laugh at him and tell him he's funny and that he's doing the right thing when maybe he isn't. Back when I played, we usually didn't have other friends besides our teammates, and we certainly didn't have an entourage to tell us how funny or how good-looking we were. We spent time with our teammates when we went out, which meant there was a little more accountability and a little less opportunity to get into the kind of trouble that players get into today. We also had no agents to cover up our misdeeds . . . or money to afford any misdeeds in the first place.

Lombardi and Landry benefited from that higher level of accountability. From the 1960s on, society changed so radically, yet I firmly believe that their military approach, depending on how it was presented, would still work today. It would have to be modified to a degree, but both coaches were such visionary, influential people that their methods would not have to be changed that much to be applied in coaching techniques today. It's just as I told Bobby Knight when he asked me if I thought Lombardi would be successful today: the methods and approach that he and Landry employed would be effective no matter what era they were used in, because nothing about the basics of the game is any different today from the days when football was played in baseball stadiums.

CHAPTER 10

"Focus on One Game at a Time"

As I write these words, there's been a lot of uproar surrounding the situation with Redskins head coach Jim Zorn, who was first stripped of his play-calling duties, then fired at the end of the 2009 regular season. It's news that was hard for me to process, given my background in the game. On the Giants, the Maras' ownership set such high standards that looking at the Redskins situation in comparison, it seems even more deplorable. The Giants' ownership would never have done anything like that—they had such respect for their coaching staff and Jim Lee Howell. I don't think they would have brought back a guy who had been out of the game for two years to call plays, and it shocked me that the Redskins did it. I know Jim Zorn reasonably well and I know what a competitor he is. This must have just crunched on him; he had to swallow a lot of pride to handle it the way he has, by saying that he wants to be the coach there for the next ten years.

A situation like that would just never have happened on a team run by the Mara family. They had a hard time letting go of Steve Owen and Jim Lee Howell. It had to be Howell's choice to stop coaching. I know there were discussions during my time on the Giants about when Howell was going to retire and how Lombardi would be elevated to the head coach position. There always have been stories about Howell's animosity toward Lombardi and rumored jealousy, but those stories are completely unfounded. I don't know if ownership had that discussion with Landry as well, but I know they did with Howell and Lombardi about Lombardi being the heir apparent, and he would have been if he had chosen to stay.

I remember flying down to Miami for Super Bowl III, when the Jets were playing Baltimore. I went to Kennedy International Airport and flew down to the game with Wellington and Ann Mara. They were concerned about the outcome of the game, though everyone except them thought that Baltimore was a shoo-in to win the game against the Jets, including me. Ann Mara said, "I would feel a lot better if our Vinny were coaching the Colts," because, at that time, there was still resentment between the two leagues, and the Maras had a lot of doubts about Baltimore. Even though Lombardi had been with Green Bay for several years (and they had won the first two Super Bowls), he was still "our Vinny" to them. They would have felt a lot safer about the outcome of an NFL versus AFL game if he were coaching. Not to mention that the Jets were hated by Giants people anyway, since they were intruders into our territory. I think the Maras were firm believers in Landry and Lombardi's "If you do it our way, you'll win" mantra.

At the end of the '58 season, we did it their way and we were winning, just as they promised. But we were under tremendous pressure; the pressure never lets up in football. We had to beat the Browns in the final game of the regular season. We had to beat them to get the chance to beat them again in a one-game playoff. The Browns lost only twice all year, and one of those losses had been to us, so we knew the situation.

When preparing us for that final game, I don't remember Lombardi or Landry changing their approach in any way or ratcheting things up. It was a lot of emotion for them (and us) to keep under the vest. If anything, I think both of them approached that game with a more composed nature, trying to calm us down, because we were very aware of the situation and what we had to do, and we had Jim Brown in our heads, riling us up. Nevertheless, I don't recall the coaches making an emphatic point of talking about him. We obviously already knew who he was and what we had to face from him, especially our defense.

We focused on only one game at a time. Of course we understood that we'd play them again in Yankee Stadium in the playoffs if we beat them this time, but that wasn't something we dwelled on too much. We focused on the first game and the task at hand. Actually, we didn't even consider the second game. I know it's an ultimate sports cliché to say we took it one game at a time, but that's really how it was approached.

Then game day arrived . . . and on the first play from scrimmage that Cleveland ran, Jim Brown ran sixty-five yards for a touchdown and we couldn't get him down. You can't imagine the air coming out of the balloon like it did after that first play. Brown just ran up the middle of the field. Nobody had a real shot at him. I remember after that happened, Landry called the defensive unit together and told them what happened. We had a little meeting on the sidelines and went over what we had to do. He emphasized the philosophy of "do it my way," as we all expected him to do. The fact that Brown had run sixty-five yards on the first series of downs made us realize that we had to tighten up a lot. We held it pretty much under control for the rest of the game; that was their last touchdown.

It was not unusual for Landry to call meetings on the sidelines. If someone scored against us, he would frequently follow that procedure of talking about what had happened and what we needed to do differently, but never calling anyone out.

That was really the game that built Sam Huff. It was the start of his vendetta against Jim Brown. That's the kind of thing that doesn't show up in the box score, as the expression goes—the game within the game. After that play, Brown had 148 yards total, including that 65-yard touchdown, which meant that he got only 83 yards for the rest of the day. That was still a big accomplishment in those days, but whatever Landry said did the trick.

There was always a calmness to him. "Come on, let's settle down. Let's do our job. Let's do what we're supposed to do," he would say, and the unit would perform as it was supposed to perform. Other coaches didn't have that gift at all. A typical coach might rant and rave or chew individual players out. He might take his linebacker and tell him what he didn't do, chew him out, and say that he had to be more intense, which is self-defeating because players already feel bad enough when the opposition scores. That was just not Landry's nature, though, nor the way he coached.

I see plenty of coaches today running up and down the sidelines, ranting and raving. There is a conflict today between a coach's need to coach and say what needs to be said to his players, and his need to perform so he is the face of the team. Because of television and the media's invasion into the inner circle, there is always a quest for more information on what makes the coach tick; the focus has shifted to analyzing the individual but not the team. In many cases, today's coaches think they have to present a sort of image on the sidelines, because they know they are surrounded by cameras. They are hyperconscious of what the public sees as a result of this invasion of the cameras. How they conduct themselves on the sidelines becomes more and more of a theater as years pass, and they become more concerned with their image and portrayal of what a head coach is supposed to do.

During our game against Cleveland, we were already high enough anyway, because we understood the pressure of the situation. At the time and in those circumstances, Landry's calm demeanor was an asset. That calmness can get a coach fired today, though—and it very well might in Dallas. When you see Wade Phillips on the sidelines, he looks bewildered, as though he doesn't know what's going on around him. I know for a fact that the newspapers here in Dallas portray him as a simpleton who doesn't really understand the game and who has been successful only because of the people around him. I know him so well and I know he understands the game; it's only that he doesn't appear to be in the action. I think that's just who he is: he is a man with a calm nature and a puzzled look on his face. Of course, he's been told he needs media training. They write it in the paper every day. Even in his press conferences, his personality still projects the image of "I'm not sure what happened or why it happened." He cares, I know he cares, about the fact that people are saying "Why are you so detached?" He says he doesn't care, but I know he does. He just doesn't project the image of somebody who is a big motivator.

I still believe the head coach has to be a motivator. It's his primary job if he's surrounded by all the support and the assistants they have today. He has to lead the team—and project the appearance of leadership. You wouldn't know Jim Zorn was in charge in Washington, for example. His demeanor is not as severe as Wade Phillips's is, but one gets the impression he doesn't know why they called a time-out or how many time-outs they have left. He reflects doubt, not motivation, in the way he conducts himself on the sidelines.

Landry's calm demeanor, on the other hand, had a very powerful effect on the team and in settling down the defensive unit. His attitude never changed on the sidelines, even through all the years he was head coach of the Cowboys. Everyone always got that same stoic figure on the sidelines who had coached the team, gotten them in shape, and gotten them ready. He always presented calm self-confidence and a blank exterior. It could be nerve-racking never knowing where we stood with him, but it was a relief to have that calmness under pressure like what we experienced playing the Browns. Because we had gotten so high off anxious energy, knowing the situation that faced us, and because of what had happened with Jim Brown on the first play, we absolutely needed that calm surface. It was necessary at that moment to get us up from that emotional low and get us back to doing what we were supposed to do.

It's fair to say that Landry's calmness contributed to the difference in the rest of the game. It was incredibly frustrating for Brown to make a touchdown like that after all we had done in practice. But we still had to play. If we had had someone at the helm who was more concerned about camera coaching, things might have ended differently that day.

When I was broadcasting, we knew who the emotional coaches were, the leaders who stood out in front, the ones who wore the headsets, and so on. You look at Tom Coughlin in New York, for instance, and he looks like he's not quite sure what's going on. He does know, believe me, but he's not ranting and raving on the sidelines. The coach's conduct reflects itself in the way the team plays; at least that's the way the analyst approaches it. It may not be true, but you'll hear it time and again from the analyst. So coaches may say they're not interested in the cameras, but every one of them is aware that they're being scrutinized. I learned that as a broadcaster by watching them and from their remarks in private. They would say, "Why did you say that? Why do you have to get inside my head? Why do you think you have to know what I'm thinking? Why do you think you *know* what I'm thinking?" And I'd have to respond with, "That was just my feeling." You have to be honest.

I remember when Bill Parcells replaced Ray Perkins as Giants head coach. Perkins called John Madden and me into the room where he was staying. They were playing the Eagles and staying in Cherry Hill. He asked us, "Have you guys met the coach who's going to take my place?" and we both said, "No, we haven't." He opened the door and brought Parcells in and said to him, "These are two guys you can trust," which is about as fine a compliment as a head coach ever paid me. By his comment, I think he meant, "These are two guys you can tell what you're going to do, the mood of the team, et cetera, and they'll keep it to themselves. They won't betray a confidence." That's what I took him to mean.

Everybody nowadays thinks they have an angle—that's the difference between the media today and when we played. The writers traveled with us. We got to be friends with them. They saw us on the practice field. They didn't talk to us during practice, but afterward, if we were at a bar and talking with friends, say, on the staff of the *New York Herald Tribune* or the *New York Journal American*—some of the papers that were in existence then but that no longer exist—they wouldn't violate a confidence. They had the same sort of trust in us (and we in them) that Ray Perkins was talking about as he introduced us to Parcells. They were not looking for their own angle, as they are today: their own little inside tidbit, their own story. There wasn't that competition between media outlets that there is today.

Competition within the media affects the way the game is coached and played. Players today have to be very careful about what they say about another player or coach, because they know it's going to end up in print. I think it has affected Roy Williams here in Dallas. He can do no right. Everybody thinks it was a mistake for the Cowboys to trade the rights to their first, third, and sixth round draft picks for him, and they let it be known by writing it in the papers. Troy Aikman has said on the air, in fact, that it had to go down as the worst trade in the history of the franchise. I don't know what there is between Roy Williams and him or if there is indeed anything, but he says the guy doesn't run his patterns correctly and that he's out of shape. Those are the kinds of things that today's papers will get into that they never would have in my day.

Back then, we had a coach whose calm disposition helped quiet the emotions of his team, get us back to his plan, and eventually shut down the Browns. Today, in that same situation, a coach would have to be concerned about how he appears to the media and to the world. It would be just as important as what he tells his players to do to win the game. The media are looking for something to comment on and competing with each other for insider commentary, and if a coach gets caught up in worrying about impressions, he's not going to be very successful for very long.

The emphasis on appearance for an insecure coach can be detrimental to his career. He has to put it out of his mind if he's going to battle with the realities of coaching and have any degree of success. Look, again, at Tom Coughlin on the sidelines. It seems like he's never sure of what's going on, yet he has a reputation as a disciplinarian and a tough guy. He very famously went from being a martinet in his early years with the team, someone the players called "Colonel Coughlin," to loosening up and becoming more approachable—and earning the team even greater success and a Super Bowl title, possibly as a result. He not only became more approachable with the team, but evened out his media manner as well; he's very careful what he says in his press conferences about the condition of the team. I think that because of this, the Giants, who are notoriously patient with head coaches, have given him a long-term contract. And, of course, the fact that he won a Super Bowl for them counts for a lot.

The reality is that a lot of desperate teams will throw money at the doors of coaches who have won Super Bowls, so the franchise with whom they won the Super Bowl has to pay them a lot and give them a long-term contract to keep them. A great example of this dynamic is Bill Belichick, whose martinet style might rub people the wrong way—were it not for his three Super Bowl wins. His protégé Eric Mangini, on the other hand, is vilified for the exact same coaching style in both New York and Cleveland, because he hasn't won a title to back him up.

The New York media are louder but not necessarily more knowledgeable. Giants receiver Steve Smith, after they won the Super Bowl, said that the reason they were able to win on the road was because the home fans were so terrible to them that they couldn't concentrate. It was only on the road that they were able to focus and win, including in the playoffs. My experience with New York fans is that they are similar to New York media. I go back to the statement John Madden made: "If they ever understand what we're talking about, we're in a hell of a lot of trouble." I think many New York fans make a louder noise because there are more of them who think they are more knowledgeable, due to the fact that there are more print and news media in New York.

But I've always found Giants fans to be a very loyal group. They certainly were at that game back in 1958. Jim Brown's first run had a quieting influence on them. After all, people were just getting settled in their seats. It took the air out of the crowd, and it took a long time for them to get involved in the game again. And what a good game it was.

There was no more scoring in the first quarter, so obviously whatever Landry said helped. In the second quarter, Lou Groza and I traded field goals, with me kicking a forty-six-yarder. There was no scoring during the third quarter. It was an extremely tense affair. I don't recall Landry or Lombardi saying anything of major consequence. We all got so wrapped up in the game itself. They wouldn't have needed to anyway; they had given us directions and we knew what we had to do.

In the fourth quarter, we had an eight-yard pass from Gifford to Bob Schnelker. It was an option pass, and we had used it during the year because Gifford could throw the ball, so it was not a total surprise to the Browns. Then I had my famous forty-nine-yard field goal, after which Lombardi came up to me and said, "You son of a bitch, you can't kick it that far!" I never saw him like that before, not with me or with anyone else.

Before the field goal, I had been hoping for a first down so they wouldn't ask me to kick. There had been a fumble on third down, though, and that meant I had to go out. As I mentioned before, the teammate who dropped a pass on third down said to me many, many times after that, "If I had caught that ball on third down, nobody would have ever heard of you." I'd go so far as to say that I probably never would have been hired by CBS and never gotten into broadcasting if he had caught that ball; I truly believe that.

I wasn't able to kick off because I was hurt from the week before. We had beaten Detroit in Detroit. I had gotten hit on a kickoff and had a bad, bad bruise. There was some question before the game if I could even kick extra points. I hadn't kicked all week in practice, but as I warmed up before the game, it started to loosen up and feel better. I told Jim Lee Howell that I would be okay to kick all field goals and extra points, but probably not to kick off.

I was hoping that a first down before my forty-nine-yard field goal would either keep the drive going or make it a shorter field goal. Even though I had already kicked a forty-six-yard field goal and an extra point in the game, I still wasn't very confident at all. I went out with doubt in my mind, and when I went out to the huddle, Charlie Conerly, our quarterback and holder, said, "What the hell are you doing here?" That doesn't build confidence.

In that day and at that time, rules weren't what they are now, as far as bringing the ball back to the spot of the kick. So the worst-case scenario wasn't missing it, but shanking it or getting it blocked. It didn't take the pressure off, though. We needed to win to force a playoff. A tie wouldn't have been good enough. In those days, there was no sudden death in the regular season, so a punt wouldn't have been as good as a field goal in this case. A tie would have put Cleveland in the playoffs against Baltimore.

Conerly clearly was not happy to see me. Maybe he thought he would be allowed to go for it with the game on the line. His attitude seemed to me to be a vote of no confidence. Lombardi didn't want to try it; he wanted to go for the first down. Howell overrode him, though, in one unusual instance of his doing something more than keeping track of time.

We had a field goal team—big guys, such as Rosey Grier and Andy Robustelli, and a lot of the other bigger and stronger defensive players were on the team to protect the kicker. As we went out, I wasn't thinking about my bad leg at the time. I wasn't thinking about the heavy snow that had begun to fall over the field. I just knew what I had to do. When I first got onto the field and Conerly asked me what the hell I was doing there, I thought, "They sent me here to try a field goal, obviously," but I didn't say that to him. I just said, "We're trying for a field goal." I don't remember thinking about the distance or my leg. I remember thinking it was totally quiet. I'm sure it wasn't, but it was one of those capsule moments when one blocks everything else out. I knew when I hit the ball that I had hit it solidly enough to get it there and that distance was not going to be a factor. But I knew it could behave a bit like a knuckleball, and I wasn't sure when it got to the goalpost if it was going to break in or break out.

For a long field goal, a kicker is supposed to swing everything at the same tempo, like when playing golf. He also has to be conscious of the distance and hit it correctly for it to get there. I remember being conscious that I had to kick it as hard as I could. Conerly said to me, "Keep your head down," as he always did before the snap, because kickers are inclined to raise their heads and look to see where the ball is going—again, the same as in golf. I didn't see any laces on the ball, so what we practiced must have come out okay.

I saw a guy standing behind the goalpost and can still see him there, with his arms outstretched, waiting to catch the ball in the back of the end zone.

We won a tense, tight game, and everything Lombardi and Landry had promised us about doing it their way came true. After the field goal, Lombardi came over and yelled about me not being able to kick it that far, whereas Landry maintained his cool composure, offering no congratulations. By then, though, I knew not to take it personally.

CHAPTER 11

Consistency Can Be a Blessing or a Curse

It's a football cliché to talk about our 1958 championship game against the Baltimore Colts as the "Greatest Game Ever Played." We certainly didn't feel that way at the time because we certainly hadn't played *our* greatest game—we weren't in peak condition. And at the time, as you'll see, people didn't realize that the game would change the course of NFL history, as has often been claimed. As we played the game, we weren't especially aware of the fact that there was a large national audience for the game on TV. In today's world of Super Bowl hype, it's hard to imagine that most of the country couldn't have cared less about the NFL's existence. That's how it was, though. The NFL at that time occupied about as much attention of the average American as does Major League Soccer today.

So in this chapter, I'd like to debunk the myths about the "Greatest Game" and offer some perspective that I haven't seen elsewhere. But before we even got to the championship, we still had to beat the Browns again. So let's start the story there.

We did put in some new plays for that game. There was a pitch from Frank Gifford back to Charlie Conerly, in which Gifford came back to trail him on the sweep call—that was a little different. Conerly ran ten yards for a touchdown on that special play. We ran a sweep to the left, and normally the quarterback brought the ball back to the halfback, and he just continued to run the sweep. But in that game, Gifford ran the sweep, and we ran a variation of the split T option play, which was the vogue in college back then. Gifford became the quarterback and pitched back to Conerly, who ran in for the touchdown after giving the appearance that he was through with the ball. He did that by sort of loafing like quarterbacks do after they hand the ball off.

It was a play we had never run before. Lombardi put it in the previous week's practice because Gifford and Conerly both came to him with that suggestion. He was very open if you had an idea that might work; Landry, not as much. Other than that new play, however, they made no changes. They retained the same kind of approach, preparation, everything. They had their "do it our way" method, and again it worked.

We totally shut them down, winning 10–0; Jim Brown had one long kick return, and the longest return for him was a forty-one-yarder, but other than that, he was unable to do anything. That game was the second building block for Sam Huff and his renown. The papers and the people who were supposedly "in the know" built the playoff up as a Sam Huff versus Jim Brown game. It was true: if you stopped Brown, you pretty much had them stopped. They had other weapons, but nothing like him, so Lombardi and Landry's emphasis going in that week was on stopping Jim Brown.

We stopped him, all right. He rested a few plays because of injury and the backup fullback, Dick Modzelewski, played a little bit. I think that was one of the few times, maybe one of the only times, that Jim Brown ever left a game for a physical reason.

In the second quarter I had a twenty-six-yard field goal, and that was the end of all the scoring in the game. The rest of it was just about holding them and the defense concentrating on Jim Brown. They had another good back besides Jim Brown, named Bobby Mitchell, but he wasn't a factor. None of them was really able to do much on offense.

Although the Browns were our biggest rivals, I didn't really think the outcome of that third game was surprising. I had thought, "We beat these guys twice. Why can't we do it again?" I think everyone had thought that. But we weren't laid-back in our approach to the game because of that. We just knew that these were the guys we had to handle.

As we prepared for it, our approach stayed the same, as it always did. Lombardi and Landry's demeanor didn't change, either. That was one of the great things about both of them. In Paul Hornung's book, *Lombardi and Me*, there are interviews with players and coaches who worked with Lombardi in Green Bay. One of the things that came across from those interviews was how caustic and hurtful Lombardi could be at practices; he would tear people down on the field and build them up in private. I found that to be true for his time with the Giants as well. That attitude and the way he treated players didn't change in the playoffs or during our championship game.

I think that every coach and player, for as long as the NFL has been in business and probably in college ball, too, has always looked for consistency. I remember Joe Gibbs telling us this over and over: when it came to officiating, what he was looking for was consistency. That holds true for coaching and player performance as well. I believe that what players are looking for is a coach who remains consistent, so that his players know what to expect from him, whether it be good or bad. A player wants to know what his coach's reaction or demeanor will be in certain situations. He just wants him to be the same every day, or as near to that as he can. It's very much like parenting, in a way, and I do think that Lombardi and Landry were father figures to us.

Of course, when we were growing up, the father was a distant figure for many of us players—both metaphorically and in life. I talked about a players' coach before, and being a players' coach was one of the things those two guys avoided. There was a big gap between them and friendship. Although years later I developed friendships with both of them, there was always that fatherly, authoritarian feeling. They had the answers, they knew the routines, they had the consistency we were looking for. It was that "father knows best" gig—they might have been distant parents, but they were consistent in that sense. There were coaches who changed when everything was on the line. That level of consistency that Lombardi and Landry had is something not many coaches can achieve.

Before the championship, we had beaten the Colts in the regular season, 24–21, on a last-second field goal, so we knew how good they were. We had a lot of respect for individual players, such as Gino Marchetti. Phil King was a rookie running back for us, and he had held Marchetti in our first game. He told us, "Marchetti picked me up off the ground and said, 'You son of a bitch. You hold me again and I'll kill you.'" He couldn't believe how strong Marchetti was; King weighed about 230 pounds and Marchetti was able to pick him up all the way off the ground. We hadn't played against Johnny Unitas in that game, though. George Shaw had been the quarterback; Unitas was hurt at the time.

In our preparations for the championship, we didn't have the kind of confident mood we had the week before our game against Cleveland. We knew the Colts were a lot fresher from their extra week off than we were. Lombardi and Landry went into scouting reports in more detail, but of course, their normal approach to the game didn't waver.

I was with Colts wide receiver Raymond Berry not too long ago. ESPN went back and colorized that '58 championship, and I asked Berry, "What was your game plan back then?" He said, "The only game plan was what I heard Weeb Ewbank say to Unitas: 'Throw it, and throw it a lot.' That was the only game plan we had."

They may not have had fancy terminology, but their game plan did its job. They threw to Berry over and over again; he caught twelve passes for 178 yards and a touchdown. He was unstoppable and physically superior to our defensive back, who was trying to cover him. I think that they had figured out the keys to attacking the "Landry defense," based on my conversation with Berry a few months ago. Landry's defense was based on the philosophy of "We'll do this and we'll do it better than you can," and they certainly figured out some of the tricks Landry had in mind, such as running a particular play where, if the halfback blocks, the receiver runs it out, or having the receiver run a cut-in pass pattern if the halfback swings out of the backfield. From my conversation with Berry, it sounded as though they spent plenty of time breaking down our films. I didn't have a sense of that at the time, though. At that time, it wasn't unusual for coaches to stick to a game plan and not make significant adjustments during games, so it was pretty much the sport standard to have coaches who were better at strategy than game-time improvisation.

Lombardi and Landry handled the loss sort of matter-of-factly. They made some adjustments during the game, but they didn't work. Neither one of them was particularly good at making spur-of-the-moment adjustments during a game. If it's possible to say that either one of those legendary coaches had a weakness, that would be it. They weren't "game time" coaches, coaches who could make adjustments when the opposing team did something unexpected. They planned what they wanted to run, and they ran it.

That weakness cost us a lot in that championship. Berry had been killing one of our defensive backs, so Landry put Harland Svare in front of him. Berry and "Golden Arm" Johnny Unitas realized what was going on, so they changed the way they ran the patterns. Landry never adjusted for it, so Unitas and Berry just kept connecting. Berry's number of completions in that game is still the championship record.

But even that tendency in both men—that inability to adjust quickly—can hardly be considered a point against them. They were both so dominating during those years with the Giants and throughout their careers with the Packers and the Cowboys that it was rare that they needed to adjust quickly to an opponent's unexpected maneuver. If you're winning all the time, you don't get a lot of practice at last-minute adjustments.

When the game went into overtime, however, nobody could have predicted what to do, because that was the first-ever overtime. The Colts were fresher than we were, which makes a big difference in an overtime game. I think fatigue definitely becomes a factor. One of the things about today's game that makes it so different is that fatigue is not often a real factor. There are so many specialists who can sub in. It usually only becomes an issue nowadays during playoffs, when coaches want to play their stars as much as possible.

If you take away the line, you don't have to be the most astute football fan to pick matchups head-to-head. The line is what keeps it interesting from a betting perspective, but an underdog beating the champs in week six is relatively rare. Back then, there were elite teams—the Giants, the Colts, the Browns—but Lombardi and Landry still preached their "any given Sunday" sermon, and that's what they truly thought.

For Super Bowl III, between the Jets and the Colts, the Colts were such heavy favorites that there was a twenty-one-point spread in a lot of areas. Yet the idea of "any given Sunday" still applied. The players on each team nowadays are basically the same size and speed. They are getting paid similar salaries, going through the same weight training programs, et cetera. You end up with an organization such as the Redskins because of the quality of the organization and the coaching staff, as well as the desire to perform that the players have on a given weekend. It's the things they do internally, such as lacking consistency, that can contribute to or detract from their success, and all that begins with the head coach.

As important as the head coach is, however, when I think about the time and effort organizations spend on choosing a new head coach, it seems incredible to me. They may not spend as much money choosing a new pope as an NFL team does to choose a new head coach, and yet they will recycle guys who haven't won in one place and bring them to another city, and they don't win there, either. I think parity is terrific if you have great teams, but parity among mediocre teams is just not a great product. I've wondered if parity among mediocre teams would sell as well, but it seems that I already have my answer, since we have a lot of that today. There is a bell curve, with elite teams everyone expects to go all the way (and they do, year after year), and teams that just can't get off the bottom.

All anyone has to do to see why the teams that aren't any good aren't any good is to look at their practice facilities and the order in which they do things, as we did as broadcasters. If the practice facilities are dirty and inferior, the coaching staff is inferior; if the weight room is inferior, and so on, the team will be inferior. Yet it is getting pretty much to the stage where there is now parity in those things in the NFL, because it's a copycat league and everybody looks at one another's facilities. They look to model franchises: the teams that are successful year after year. I remember when the 49ers first built their facility. People went to look at it because it was supposed to be the best, since they were one of the best franchises at the time. There was a group that felt it was *too* nice and not conducive to playing tough football. They thought the new stadium coddled the players too much and made them soft, but that was not the case; they had a run in the 1980s and early 1990s that was envied by everybody in the league. It was a run like the Giants' back in my day.

I think it was Joe Montana who had the greatest impact on the 49ers' winning streak, though, not the new stadium. Similarly, the grandeur of Yankee Stadium was nothing compared to the effect Lombardi and Landry had on our successes. The end of the '58 season was the last time the two of them coached the Giants. We had an idea that if an opening came for a head coaching position, one of them would certainly go. We didn't think both of them would go, but we knew nothing about it at the time.

After the championship game, none of us had the sense that it would be our last time having both of them as assistant coaches. I don't remember things being any different from any other loss, except that we were all ready to go home. There were no special good-byes or thank-yous, no tearful farewells, or any other change in demeanor that I recall. Of course, there was always a letdown after a loss, but I don't think any of us were conscious that Lombardi was going to leave or that the game we just played was going to be called the Greatest Game Ever Played, possibly because none of us Giants felt like it was our greatest game. Everybody felt like we hadn't given it our best shot, and I think fatigue had a lot to do with that.

New York papers were on strike at the time, so if a paper such as the *Nashville Banner*, for instance, wanted the championship covered, they had to send somebody. The game got a lot more exposure and attention for that reason. Tex Maule, who was a writer for *Sports Illustrated*, was the one who first started calling it the Greatest Game Ever Played, and I think it just sort of stuck. A week after, the game started taking on mythic proportions, since it was the first overtime game and since it exposed the NFL to a national audience. Leading up to the game, I don't recall any feeling of heightened importance, however. It seemed like I was being bothered by the media a little bit more, but there was no media day or anything like that.

I remember before one of the Super Bowls that the 49ers were in, Bill Walsh told Madden and me that he felt very strongly about the media coverage Super Bowl losers didn't receive. He told us that if you got to the Super Bowl and lost, nobody ever talked about you. People only remember the winners; the loser of the Super Bowl was insignificant and forgotten, and he felt that was unfair, because they had worked so hard and accomplished so much to get there. He talked about it as if he resented the lack of attention that was paid to the loser, even though the 49ers were so successful. On the other hand, he had reached and lost five AFC title games as the coach of the Bengals, who then had the reputation that the Cowboys had for a while as the team unable to win the big one. That might have given him the sensitivity toward teams that are able to climb just shy of the top. I always thought that he perceived himself as the best at what he did and had the same "If you do it my way, we'll win" philosophy as Lombardi and Landry, which made them so successful with the Giants and with their future organizations.

Lombardi was the first to leave. I read it in a local paper when I got back home—the same way I learned about my trade to the Giants. I had heard rumors that he was going to Green Bay and also heard rumors the next year that Landry was going to take over the Cowboys. I remember thinking what a good choice Lombardi was as their new head coach; Green Bay wasn't much of a team at that time, and I knew Lombardi would change that. The Packers played in City Stadium, which was a high school field. We had played them many times and they were weak throughout, as I remember. I admired Lombardi so much, however, and knew what a good coach he was—we all knew that—and I knew Green Bay's weakness wouldn't hinder him. I had always thought that somebody had made a mistake by not hiring him as a head coach earlier, even though at forty-five he was considered advanced in age when he began coaching Green Bay.

I was sad to see him go. In all the offensive meetings we went to, I was never bored. Boredom can be an occupational hazard for football players; it's hard to make the presentation of how an in sweep should be blocked entertaining, but he had a way of making strategy into story. It wasn't about theoretical X's on a chalkboard; it was about real players playing a real game. When he presented a play, I felt like I was watching a tight game, and everything depended on the most minute adjustment in the formation. Suddenly he'd get to the end of the play, and everything would come together—I could see how it had to work on the field. I was always compelled to listen for that final payoff.

The following season without Lombardi was a huge change. Allie Sherman took over the offense. He just was not the dynamic person Lombardi was, and I remember the "Good-bye, Allie" banners in the stands. But Landry was no different without Lombardi. There was a leadership gap because Allie Sherman was not as strong as Lombardi, but the primary leader was still Jim Lee Howell. He still had his stopwatch and he still was the boss, no question about it. He filled any leadership vacuum left by Lombardi's absence. Landry left the next year and the Cowboys started with him in 1960, which was the same year Howell announced his plans for retirement at the end of the season.

Even though pro football was more on the map, when I went back to Florida in the off-season, there were still plenty of people who were not cognizant of it. There was not the same level of unawareness as there had been; after that famous field goal, the town I was from organized a Pat Summerall Day and had "Welcome Home, Pat" banners stretched across the street. Yet I still had people asking me, "Hey, Pat. What you been up to? Where you been all year?"

It was sort of welcome, though. People at home were the same people they had been the summer before. My friends knew I was playing pro football and saw the write-ups in the paper, but they were still the same. It's not the same today, with players living in gated communities for safety and security reasons. I would go to the golf course in the afternoon and the same bunch of guys would throw up the balls to see who was going to play together. I was treated no differently, which is very dissimilar from what goes on nowadays, I can tell you.

When people asked me what I'd been doing, I would say, "I've been playing for the Giants." A lot of people didn't follow pro football and would say, "Who are the Giants?" It's funny now, but it wasn't too funny then. I was partially responsible for my team getting to the championship game and taking part in the Greatest Game Ever Played, and all I got was, "Pat, where've you been?" In fact, I go back today and it still happens.

CHAPTER 12

Good Teachers Make You Want to Teach

Good teachers make you want to teach. Both Lombardi and Landry made such a difference in not only my playing style but also my life that I couldn't help but wonder if there were young players out there whom I could help in the same way. Over the course of my career, I ended up trying out coaching a few times, but I ultimately discovered it wasn't for me. Having had Lombardi and Landry's influence, however, did give me a keen insight into various coaching styles—and that ability to critique served me well in my broadcasting days. I still occasionally wonder if, had I chosen to coach, I might have been able to pass on the torch I was handed by Lombardi and Landry.

Even though there are certain elements of a franchise that have to change and evolve—the coaching, the players, the personnel, the systems—it's amazing how certain hallmarks hold steady over the decades. For instance, I watched the 2009 week nine game between the Pittsburgh Steelers and the Denver Broncos and recalled that even back when I played, the Steelers were a team that could beat a guy up. We had a guy, Roosevelt Brown, who was picked for the Pro Bowl and declined the chance because it would mean he had to play against the Steelers' Ernie Stautner again. Playing against him was so physically punishing, even in a game that didn't count in the standings, that he refused to line up against him if he didn't have to.

Of course, the ownership hasn't changed with the Steelers; it's still the Rooney family. I ran into Art Rooney, the owner of the

Steelers and the family patriarch, at Super Bowl III, when the Jets upset the Colts at the Orange Bowl in Miami in January 1969. I wasn't at the game as a broadcaster; I was actually sitting in the stands. Somebody had hired me to accompany a Super Bowl party. I had done some work for NBC on the pregame show, taping some stuff, but I was mainly there to be a pro football celebrity for that party, I suppose. We played a touch football game where I was the quarterback for my team and Sonny Jurgensen was the quarterback for his team.

I was in a hotel called Galt Ocean Mile, I'll never forget it, and I saw Art Rooney standing in line to check out after the game. I was checking out as well, and got in line with him. He had just fired his coach—Bill Austin, I think—and I asked him if he had found another coach. Well, first I said something like "Congratulations on a good year" to start the conversation, and then I said, "Mr. Rooney, do you have a coach yet?" He looked at me and said, "No. Do you want the job?"

I didn't get the impression that Art Rooney had any blueprint or plan for who he wanted, but I guess when he saw me, the idea made sense to him. In fact, he told me he was serious about his offer. I turned him down on the spot, saying that I wanted to stick with broadcasting and see what I could do, and he said, "Well, if you want the job, it's yours." I thought it over, but the thought process didn't last long. I knew by the time the flight home was over that it was not what I wanted to do. Then, two weeks later, they hired Chuck Noll. When I heard about it, I remember it caught my attention, because I knew Noll as one of the messenger guards for Paul Brown in Cleveland.

I had coaching experiences with the Rams and with Florida State that turned me off of the profession. Harland Svare was a good friend of mine, and he got the head coaching job with the Rams. We had made sort of a gentlemen's agreement that if he got a coaching job, he would hire me, and if I got a coaching job,

I would hire him. If I had been hired, I would have had him run the defense, because he was one of Landry's better players. I had just retired from playing when he got the job, and he made me the tight end coach and the kicking coach for the Rams. It was 1962 when I started; Merlin Olsen was a rookie and Roman Gabriel was the quarterback. I didn't know it at the time (I thought it was going to be a full-time job), but I stayed for only two weeks.

After two weeks, I decided it wasn't what I wanted to do, so I went to Dan Reeves, who owned the Rams at the time, and said, "Thank you for the opportunity, but this is not what I want to do." I didn't particularly like the change that had happened to the guy who had hired me; he went from a blue-jeans-and-sneakers kind of guy to the sort of man who wore a leisure suit. I just didn't like what he had become. I also thought the hours were too long, and I didn't see that I had a future in coaching. Danny Villanueva was the Rams' kicker, and I remember telling him, "You know, you're better than I ever was. There's not much I can do to help you."

Even though my career with the Rams was so short-lived, I had considered coaching often over the years. I had coached at Florida State when my wife was a senior there. That was in 1956. I was still playing with the Cardinals, but coached at Florida State during their spring practice. But honestly, I didn't like that coaching experience there, either. I just didn't like the regimentation of coaching or the breaking down of tape—well, film at that time. I didn't really have enthusiasm for coaching, and I also found the Florida State head coach, Tom Nugent, an odd duck. In one meeting, I remember he had us spend two or three hours talking about what kind of attire the coaches were going to wear in practice, and I thought, "This is not what it takes to build a football team—shorts and T-shirts versus football pants or sweats."

I got my first taste of coaching from that and didn't like it much. But then I joined the Giants and experienced the superior coaching of Lombardi and Landry, which made me think I might like it after all. Good teachers tend to make you want to become a teacher. But then I retired in 1961, Svare brought me in to coach the Rams, and it took only two weeks to change my mind back again. During that 1958 season, however, I saw Lombardi and Landry teaching, and the thought crossed my mind that I'd like to do that someday—to be as commanding as Lombardi was and as attention-holding as they both were in the way they taught.

I thought that maybe if I could portray things the way Lombardi could, if I could get the message across like he did, then that might be something I'd want to do. Plus, coaching really was the only thing I was qualified to do. I had other business interests, as well as teaching experience, but they were not things I'd want to build a career around. The upside of coaching was that I would get to lead and inspire; the downside was the long meetings on both the Rams and at Florida State, going round and round in circles without getting anything decided.

Even if I had been able to have the job on my terms, without long, indecisive meetings or the level of regimentation, I'm still not sure the job would have appealed to me. Meetings seemed like an obligation, whether we had anything to discuss or not. I don't remember ever going to a meeting with Lombardi and Landry and getting the feeling that we were just there to kill time. None of them called meetings for the sake of calling meetings; their meetings were always about finding a way to improve.

Perhaps if I had been in a better position as an NFL coach, it might have been more appealing. I might have had a more active role in shaping the team and the organization. Every coach I ever talked to asked that things be done consistently. As I mentioned earlier, I remember Joe Gibbs saying that all he wanted from his team was consistency and all he wanted from the officials was consistency. He just liked things to be done at the same level of performance and with the same level of desire. If I had ever been a head coach, I think that would have been the philosophy of my coaching career, as it was for Landry and Lombardi.

At the same time, I know it would have been tough for me to be hard on players. And I don't know of any successful head coach who isn't, when it's called for. They've all had to be tough at one time or another, even in the cases of their superstars. That's why I say that is a parallel between coaching and raising children. For example, so many parents vow that they're never going to yell at their children. Then, in the heat of the moment, their emotions take over and all those vows disappear. I think that happens between coaches and players as well. It's easy to go in with a plan of what to do and what not to do, but you never know if your plan will hold until you're under pressure.

Landry, certainly, is famous for the emotional distance he maintained as a coach. Yet I think because of my own nature, I would have been more like Lombardi. When I was practice-teaching, I coached a basketball team and I turned into a totally different character. I was yelling on the sideline, and if something happened as a result of a lack of execution, I turned into a completely changed man. Witnessing myself like that was also one of the reasons I decided not to pursue coaching—because of what it did to me. That other side of myself surprised me, and I wasn't happy with it. It was a side of me that I wasn't very proud of.

As a coach, you have to be able to be able to be happy with your own performance, as well as with that of your players. You have to know how to handle guys like Larry Johnson or even Terrell Owens, who is a very talented player but who also has given many people cause to be concerned about his emotional maturity or his ability to be a team player. Because T.O. and Larry Johnson are very talented, it would be easy for coaches to be inconsistent in how they treat them. They give them more rope than they would just a regular player. That's the quicksand of coaching.

In T.O.'s case, every coach thinks he's the one who can handle him correctly and get the best out of him. I had breakfast with one of the assistant coaches when T.O. was in Dallas and was told that he went through a training camp where he didn't really practice hard. He spent most of the time riding a stationary bike on the sidelines. The coaching staff under Bill Parcells had decided that Owens worked so hard in practice, that his work ethic was so serious and dedicated, that he burned himself out and had nothing left. So they had him on a stationary bike, not participating in practice, so he wouldn't overwork himself. They didn't tell the media or anyone else that, but that's the way they approached it.

As I said before, if a guy has superior talent, there probably are ways in which you have to treat him differently. But I would never show that, particularly to the individual who was being treated that way. That's what the Cowboys got trapped doing with Terrell Owens. Ultimately it didn't work and they had to get rid of him. I don't know if the other teams, the Philadelphia Eagles or San Francisco, tried to make things work that way with him, by getting him not to work out so seriously, but I think any coach would be tempted to do that.

I don't know if I would make allowances like that in practice when it came to handling superstar players, although I do hope I would find a way to resolve things with consistency. I would hope to handle disciplinary issues the same way. Off-the-field behavioral issues in my era were not of the same magnitude as they are today—whether it's Plaxico Burress with a handgun, Michael Vick with his dogfights, or scenes outside bars or strip clubs at 3:00 A.M. Discipline was easier in the time when I played because nobody had any money, and if we had the time, we couldn't afford to get into trouble. There were incidents and there were characters, but they didn't have the mobility or the money that today's players have. That's really where the trouble comes in.

We did have discrepancies in contracts, but not to the extent that they have today.

As I've said about the 1958 Giants, once you were in practice or on the field, you forgot about the money. I think that's one of the things teams strive to overcome today: that there is a moneyed part of the team and another part of the team that just doesn't have the same means. It's impossible to ignore because of the off-the-field lifestyles. A big story in Dallas was that the Cowboys had a week off before the playoffs and their starting quarterback, Tony Romo, went to Cabo St. Lucas with Jessica Simpson. Back in the days when I played, nobody had the means to do that. It's a nice kind of problem to have, but the fans and the media didn't think so. The big question around Dallas was what Peyton Manning would have done with that week off. I heard that mentioned several times. He would have studied, I'm sure, and gotten himself ready for the next game. The news of Romo's doings went far beyond Dallas. In fact, the *New York Post* hired a Jessica Simpson look-alike and bought her a field-level ticket just to distract the Cowboys.

If my quarterback pulled a stunt like that I would hope that, first of all, he would tell me what his plans were. If I heard he was going to go on a trip, I would have told him not to do it. If he went ahead and did it, I'd have to suspend him or fine him severely, even though it was before the playoffs. That's part of being consistent. If I said, "Don't do that. Stay here and look at film," and he defied me openly, there would have to be consequences. That seems to me to be the only way to handle it, but the administration didn't do that in this case. They let him go to Mexico and then play, and they lost.

If Wade Phillips had benched Tony Romo, if the backup had come in, taken the snaps in practice, and started as quarterback, they probably wouldn't have gotten a worse result than the loss they had with Romo as quarterback. If Romo was unprepared, then why not do that? That's one of the dilemmas coaches have. If they have somebody who is talented, as Romo is, and they want to win the game, it's a tough call. If Romo gave you a better chance to win than Brad Johnson, the Cowboys' backup quarterback, what would you do? Well, I guess the answer has to be to fine Romo and let him play. And there you have it: that's how easy it is to break consistency as a coach.

But, of course, this is all hypothetical. I don't think Romo and Phillips discussed it beforehand; Romo just went. It goes to show how quickly a coach's hands can become tied and consistency can become impossible. I think Lombardi or Landry would have played Romo in the same situation. An element of pragmatism has to be involved, after all, and I think there are certain levels of talent that coaches end up having to treat differently. I hope I wouldn't have differed from Lombardi as a coach, but I don't think I would be able to treat everyone like dogs.

Players' coaches work extremely well in college settings, but they are disastrous in the NFL. It's next to impossible to strike the balance between being a decent guy who doesn't treat everyone like dogs and not falling into the trap of being a players' coach. I know when the Cowboys started their descent, the players felt that they weren't getting fair treatment from the coach. In the beginning, they always had the option to talk to the coach, Jimmy Johnson, in private, but that kind of organization doesn't seem to work. I think that in the pros it depends on the organization behind the players. It's not just the head coach, it's those who surround him, as well, and the good head coaches, such as Jim Lee Howell, surrounded themselves with those who have adopted the same philosophy as they had. In the old days, we never would have dreamed of going around Lombardi or Landry to Jim Lee Howell, because we knew that was to no avail. The same thing went for those higher than Jim Lee Howell, such as the Mara family. We wouldn't dare do something like that with them.

The end run that players make today is to the media, though, not to ownership. Ownership, for the most part, is so removed, with the exception of people such as Jerry Jones. I can say one thing about media and publicity, though: if I were a head coach, my players would definitely not be allowed to promote themselves on Twitter. At the end of the day, playing football is about being a member of a team, and any kind of media contact or social networking that allows a single player to trump the team is detrimental. I'd insist on players maintaining all team contact with the press and the public through the coach, rather than creating one-man sideshows.

As head coach I don't think I would have followed Jim Lee Howell's model and found strong assistants and let them run things, either. I would think that I'd let my offensive coordinator call plays, with the right to disagree. I think head coaches also have to be in communication with whoever is calling plays, so they almost have to wear headsets. They have to know what's coming so they know how to evaluate key parts of the play and who's making it successful or unsuccessful. I particularly think that if a team has an offensive coordinator or a defensive coordinator, the head coach has to have knowledge of what's upcoming.

We've talked about how coaches have too much staff, but I honestly don't know what my staff would look like if I were a head coach. I don't know what quality control is, but everybody has an assistant coach who has quality control as part of his title. I do know that I would try to delegate the authority over positions and responsibilities to the appropriate assistants. I think I'd have enough confidence in myself to do that. The introduction of tape has made that especially possible, because there's something for everybody to look at. That wasn't a possibility when it was all done on film; Lombardi and Landry just didn't have the convenience of having fifteen or twenty copies of a game available.

I also hope I would have human hours as a coach. I think that as long as coaches get what work is necessary done, there's no reason on earth for them to sleep in the office or to keep an assistant until midnight every night or other extreme things that some coaches do. It's uncalled for. If a coach is efficient enough in his approach, anything beyond the call of duty is just a waste of time and a burning out of humanity.

If I had a better experience with the Rams, I very well might have been a coach. But I do think coaching would have been the wrong direction for me. My entry to broadcasting came when I was still playing, in 1960, and if my broadcasting career hadn't had signs of possibility, I probably would have taken coaching more seriously.

In preparing for a game as a broadcaster, I've found that the mechanical part of broadcasting, especially being a play-by-play man, requires more attention to time and detail than any other aspect of football I've experienced. During the week there is less regimentation as a broadcaster but not less preparation. The preparation is just a different kind. I had to learn about the players, yes, but I had to go beyond that to accentuate what they *were capable of doing*, what made them special. If there was something good about a player, I concentrated on that. I focused on the things they did well, not the things they didn't do well, and so my broadcasts had a positive feel to them. I remember thinking, "Hey, all these guys are pretty good or they wouldn't be playing in the NFL." As a head coach I know I'd be much more responsible for considering what they couldn't do as well as what they could do.

When Art Rooney asked me to coach the Steelers, the experiences I'd had with the Rams and with Florida State did not make me eager for more. I knew I felt comfortable with broadcasting and thought it was something I could do, but you better believe I still looked at the Steelers on the field in the 1970s and thought, "That could have been my team." As I said, they hired Chuck Noll two weeks after the Orange Bowl, and I watched him operate and win those Super Bowls. I looked at the people he had: the Franco Harrises and the Terry Bradshaws and the Lynn Swanns. I wondered on occasion if I would have drafted those people and how I would have put that team together. I read recently that Rooney also had offered the job to Joe Paterno, then—and now—the head coach at Penn State. I wonder whether Joe ever looked at the Steelers in the 1970s and had the same thought I did—that he could have been their coach.

Part of the success of the Steelers was the strength of their drafts. The way they put that team together is legendary. I've wondered, "Would I have approached it that way? Would Terry Bradshaw have been my quarterback?" When he was drafted, there were teams that thought he was not smart enough to lead a professional team, though he had physical ability. In fact, I think the Giants were thinking about drafting him—but as a tight end, not as a quarterback.

When I asked myself those questions back then, I think they were unanswerable. I don't know what I would have done. Would I have drafted Mean Joe Greene? Would I have taken Dwight White and all those other talented people the Steelers drafted? I don't know, I still don't know, and I never will know. They obviously built a dynasty and they were one of the most exciting teams and still are. Their consistency is due to the fact that the ownership hasn't changed; Bill Cowher was different from Mike Tomlin in his approach and coaching.

I talked over the Steelers possibility with Madden, but I don't remember that those discussions lasted very long. He was of the opinion that I should have gotten into coaching because he had and because he had such success with it. However, I think his health suffered because of it. He developed an ulcer because of his devotion to detail and his rigorous adherence to consistency, and I think that's why he got out of coaching. At the age of forty-two, he got out when he was on top and very young; he was only thirty-one when he started coaching the Raiders.

Yet, at that time, I thought coaching was too big a risk. And most importantly, I just didn't enjoy it—and I *did* enjoy broadcasting. If I had taken time off to try coaching, there wouldn't have been a spot for me in broadcasting; they would have moved on. So that was one line I ultimately had to draw in the sand: Lombardi and Landry's influence on me stopped at shaping my coaching career. I never followed in their footsteps that way. John Madden's attitude was that I would have been an excellent coach and he wished I would have gone into coaching, but I don't have any regrets; Chuck Noll did just fine.

CHAPTER 13

Don't Dwell on Your Success

It was obvious to me that coaching wasn't my path and that broadcasting was. Once I'd cast my line in the broadcasting waters, one thing led to another, and I had more and more opportunities. And slowly, over time, I discovered that there is a lot of teaching involved in broadcasting, just as in coaching. So, of course, I started with what I knew: football. But over time, I was able to broadcast basketball, golf, and tennis as well, but even as I strayed from football, I continued to feel Lombardi and Landry's influence on my professional path. They taught me to have the confidence and coolness under pressure it takes to go in front of an audience of millions day after day, and more importantly, they taught me how to communicate effectively. Even if I didn't follow in their coaching footsteps, I ultimately came to feel that I had followed in their teaching footsteps.

I discovered through whatever success I had being an NFL announcer that I wanted to continue in the broadcasting profession. I made friends with Bill MacPhail, the head of CBS Sports, and talked with him a couple of times about doing golf. Everybody who is any kind of announcer looks at the sport of golf, the glorious places they go to, and has a secret hankering to cover it. But there are only 4 majors for golf, whereas there are 162 baseball games, 16 regular-season NFL games at this writing, and an endless NBA season, so there is an elite quality to golf broadcasting and a sense that the rest of the league is watching.

I pestered Bill about it until he finally let me work at about the sixteenth hole at the Buick Open in Flint, Michigan.

Broadcasting a major golf tournament is not nearly as easy as it might appear. In fact, it is by far the toughest assignment for most sportscasters, as much as everyone wants to do it. What do you say when a guy makes a putt? "That's a birdie," or "That's a par," or "That puts him two out of the lead."

The announcer's options are limited. The same goes when a player is out on the fairway. "He's 165 yards out. He's got an eight-iron. He should come in from left to right." That's stock stuff. To enhance it, I had to be creative—take a step out. I talked about the wind, the lie, recent changes in the golfer's swing, or what he was likely discussing with his caddie. Creativity is much more difficult in golf than in many other broadcast assignments. I remember CBS's golf producer Frank Chirkinian telling me, "Television is a visual medium. You don't have to tell people what they can see. Tell them something they can't see. People can see that a golfer made the putt. If I ever hear you say, 'He made the putt,' I'll fire you on the spot."

Football was much simpler. There are twenty-two players on the field and only a finite number of things you need to keep up with: the score, the time on the clock, the down, and so on. Then you call the plays as they happen. You don't have to struggle for things to talk about because there is so much going on. Basketball's even quicker. You just follow the ball while keeping track of the ten players on the court.

The downtime is a killer in golf. I had to fill it with either brilliance or bull. When things slowed down, I sometimes had to go into a golfer's history, talk about his family and his struggles and triumphs.

I must have done a good job my first time as a golf announcer, because after the Buick Open, they told me, "Okay, you'll do the eighteenth at Augusta." There was no accolade or anything, although what more did I need? For my second golf tournament, I was going to broadcast at the 1968 Masters at the eighteenth hole, the coveted position. For the broadcasting world, doing the World Series, Super Bowl, or Masters is like finding the pot of gold at the end of the rainbow. Besides, playing under Landry had made me used to not receiving compliments for a job well done.

I had been to Augusta only once before. When I was growing up in 1945, all the regular caddies were in the service. A local druggist from Lake City somehow got an invitation to play and hired me to go to Augusta and caddie for him for fifty cents a day. I was fifteen at the time and didn't have the great reverence for Augusta that I had later in life. All I knew was that it was a tough place to walk. It was hilly and I had to carry all his equipment around the course—suffice it to say that the bag got heavy after just a hole or two. Also, the fellow I was caddying for was not a very good golfer, which made the day much longer. However, I remember feeling privileged to have the opportunity, as hard as the work was.

When I came back as a broadcaster, I was definitely struck by the beautiful mystique of that place. Cliff Roberts and golfing legend Bobby Jones Jr. co-founded the Augusta National Golf Club and built it on a 365-acre flower nursery that had served as an indigo plantation before the Civil War. I'd been on many golf courses, but I'd never seen more pristinely manicured grounds. Every tree, shrub, and blade of grass was perfect.

The Masters is better administered than any other sporting event, hands down. They take such pride in the product and it shows, not only in the way they take care of the grounds, but also in other aspects. For example, the way the fans—they call them patrons—are treated. The folks at the Masters make sure that parking is stress-free and that the prices of sandwiches, drinks, and other concessions are incredibly reasonable, along with the wait time. I once overheard one of the tournament organizers say, "Well, last year in the pimento-cheese sandwich line, it took an average of three minutes to get through. We better cut that down. We need to sell it in more places." Furthermore, everything is wrapped in green, and you never see garbage or debris lying on the ground, which is partly due to the respect the patrons have for the place. They say you can arrive when the gates open at six thirty, put your chair by the eighteenth hole, leave to walk the course, come back later, and your chair will be undisturbed in the spot you left it. The manners of the patrons are such that the entire experience is remarkable.

Because the tournament in Augusta is built not only around the gorgeous landscape but also around the traditions of respect and graciousness, the chairmen make sure that they control everything with an iron fist. I knew about the reputation of Cliff Roberts going into the tournament. There never had been a contract between CBS and the Augusta National, and there still isn't. It's just a handshake, which is unheard of in televised sports, and CBS bent over backward to make sure that they made Roberts happy and didn't lose the prestigious event. They bowed to every demand: CBS wasn't allowed to expand its coverage of the Masters, as it had for the U.S. Open and other majors, and we had to limit commercial content and get final approval for all commercial content from the Masters Tournament office.

As a broadcaster, we also were given a dos and don'ts list of things we could say on the air. We could not make any references to money or how much the prize was, we had to make sure to call it the venue Augusta National Golf Club, not a country club, we couldn't talk about how one gets to be a member   efer to membership at all, and we couldn't mention the bran   oes or clothes a player was wearing. This, obviously, is not   NFL broadcasting, and at first it made me feel very rest   n the topics I could talk about. This code of broadcasting   true for the Masters, and after a while I got used to it.

I remember one CBS announcer forgot himself—at least in the eyes of Roberts—and paid the price. In 1966, Jack Whitaker referred to the crowd at a Monday playoff between Gene Littler and Billy Casper as a "mob" that had left behind an inordinate amount of "garbage." Roberts and the Augusta brass took exception to this and banned Jack from future coverage. The Masters didn't have a "mob," they had "patrons," CBS was told. Nor did they have "garbage"; they had "debris." And who could forget Gary McCord getting ousted as a commentator for saying the greens looked bikini-waxed? In the end, the joke was on Augusta—McCord ended up with a groundswell of fan support.

You can bet I made sure that I stuck to the code during my broadcast. The eighteenth hole is a cherished position at any golf tournament for a broadcaster; it's basically the host position. I was on my own in the eighteenth tower and Chirkinian told me, "The important part of any broadcast is that you bring it on the air and you take it off." That was my responsibility, and whether it was because of my performance, I was moved back subsequent years to the fourteenth, thirteenth, eleventh, tenth holes, and so on. I didn't question why they moved my hole coverage back, but I could certainly see the difference and it rankled a little bit.

At the start of the 1968 Masters, I went with Frank Glieber, who was from Dallas, to the practice putting green to learn a bit about the other players. I played golf and followed it in the papers. I was familiar with who Nicklaus, Palmer, and Player were, but I didn't have a great knowledge of the other golfers and knew I had a lot of homework to do. There was a British player on the putting green who I didn't know much about and Frank didn't know anything about. He had a golf bag that had the name "Slazenger" on the side, which is a British sporting goods company. I remember Frank pointing and saying, "What do you know about that guy Slazenger over there?" and I said, "Frank,

that's not the name of the golfer, that's a sporting goods company!"
So I wasn't alone in my first-time jitters.

For the Masters, each person had a living assignment. Instead
of staying at a hotel, we all stayed in houses that were rented from
people in Augusta. My roommates, Bob Dailey, one of the directors, and Frank Chirkinian, were all as honored as I was to be part
of the broadcast, but most of them had been there before, so they
were not quite as awestruck as I was. I had no idea how much my
newbie nerves were going to be tested, though.

On Sunday, Roberto De Vicenzo, a popular Argentine player,
signed an incorrect scorecard. His playing partner, Tommy Aarons,
mistakenly put down a "4" instead of a "3" at the seventeenth
hole. When he got to the eighteenth hole, we had his score
down as one stroke less, and when he walked off the eighteenth
green, I said something on the air like, "There's our champion,"
in acknowledgment that he was going to win the tournament.
During the next commercial, Chirkinian talked to me using a
special apparatus that we had and said, "Don't say who won on
the air." I was incensed, because I thought it was clear that he had
won, and asked him why. He said that there might be a problem
with his scorecard, but didn't give me any other information.

At that time, the scorer's tent where players signed their score-
cards was right behind the eighteenth green. They've moved it
now to another location because of this incident. Anyway, that
was all I knew for a long while—that there might be a problem.
As time progressed, of course I didn't mention the winner again,
and then Bob Goalby came in and won the tournament.

I didn't understand what was happening at the time, but De
Vicenzo had looked at the card in the scoring area, signed it, and
had Aarons attest to it. The officials recorded the score he signed
for, and that was the score that stood. Goalby birdied the seventeenth
or eighteenth hole to win the Masters. If the officials had let De
Vicenzo get away with the mistake, he and Goalby would have

had an eighteen-hole playoff the next day. However, Goalby was declared the winner.

I saw him years later and talked with him for a long time about it. He felt that he never quite got the credit he deserved for being a champion. With De Vicenzo signing an incorrect scorecard, most of the publicity about that tournament went to De Vicenzo, not Goalby. Many newspapers and fans felt that Goalby didn't really win the tournament and that he sort of won by default. He took a lot of flak from reporters and fans. He eventually got a letter from Bobby Jones saying that he won the Masters fair and square. He never won another Masters, though.

Before I knew all this, however, I was stuck in the eighteenth tower, talking about a game whose winner I couldn't mention. Believe me, it was a bizarre turn of events. I remember Chirkinian telling me not to talk about it anymore and being angry that I had done the wrong thing, but the rest of that day is a blank to me. I don't remember how we covered it. For about a half-hour period, they went into Bobby Jones's cabin to talk it over. None of the broadcasters were informed about what was going on; we were told the event was over, but not to talk about who won—not that we had any idea. I remember thinking, "Here I am on the eighteenth. It's my first Masters and now they're telling me not to say what I think is the truth." I had been an NFL broadcaster for six years, but I still had no clue what to do or how to handle myself. Frankly, I don't remember what went on. I knew there was a problem with the scorecard, which I wasn't supposed to mention, and that was the extent of my knowledge.

That was one of the longest half-hours of my life. There were people milling around who were reluctant to leave. They weren't sure if there was going to be a playoff. There were rumors of the mistake—we heard about Goalby before the official word came. We also got word that De Vicenzo kept saying, "I am a stupid. I am a stupid." I don't recall if I reported that at the close of the broadcast, but when I got the news from Chirkinian, I made the announcement before we went off the air.

I didn't know much about De Vicenzo at the time, except that he was the darling of Argentina and had the reputation of being a tough competitor and a gentleman, a player who belonged in the ranks of Player, Palmer, and Nicklaus in terms of talent. Goalby, on the other hand, was also an ex-football player. He was a quarterback at Illinois. He always remained sort of bitter because he didn't get the credit he thought he should have for winning a Masters. He was cognizant that he won because of a mistake, but still thought people should have recognized the fact that he played extremely well.

His performance and the whole event were things I talked about many, many times later. Because it was my first Masters, people continuously ask me about it during discussions. When they ask me when my first Masters was and I answer "1968," I always clarify it with "You know, the year Roberto De Vincenzo signed the incorrect scorecard," because that's how everyone remembers that Masters. People continue to talk about it today. When I'm sitting around with a group at Augusta, it inevitably comes up.

There is no question that I benefited greatly from my exposure to Landry and Lombardi and from the pressure of playing for the Giants. I don't know if I handled the broadcasting situation at the Masters with grace, especially since I don't remember much of what I said, but I know that I felt pressure like that before and handled it better than I would have because of my association with Lombardi and Landry. I didn't go back to the eighteenth hole in the broadcast, though, so I'm sure CBS and the people at the Augusta National didn't think I did a very good job. Whatever happened after Chirkinian said, "Don't say who won on the air," cost me my ability to go back to the eighteenth hole the next year and for many years to come.

I was lucky, though, that I was at least asked back for subsequent years. Tony Trabert and Tom Brookshier were golf broadcasters who were not asked back after slipups. There were some people on the 1968 broadcast who didn't do a good enough job to be asked back as well. Funnily enough, even though everybody wanted to do golf, most of the guys who were on broadcast golf were nonprofessionals and not very good golfers themselves. We had a guy, Ken Venturi, involved with the Masters who was a pro golfer, we could call him in if we had to ask about a ruling or had a question. It wasn't like it is now, with a guy following a group around. We had an announcer at almost every hole from the first to the eighteenth. It was not as extensive as it is now, with people covering both the front and back nine, because the equipment today is so much more mobile.

Because of a lack of instant communication and uncertainty, what could have been a great experience and a real accomplishment—broadcasting from the eighteenth hole at my first Masters—turned out to be a demotion for me, kind of putting me in the same boat as De Vicenzo. I had no idea what was happening on the ground or how long I would have to cover until they announced the champion. Until that final round, the Masters people and CBS had been satisfied with my performance. Who knew that the winner of the tournament would end up on the list of unmentionable topics? If I hadn't learned grace under pressure from my two coaches, I'm sure I would have handled everything much worse than I did.

As I said, Lombardi and Landry's influence and the experience of being in pressure situations with the Giants helped me in everything I did. Lombardi, particularly, had an influence on the way I broadcast, because I was so impressed by his oratory. Landry never really said anything much; Lombardi was the more dynamic with the way he presented things. What he said and the way he said it stuck with me. My interest in broadcasting came from being around him and from the effectiveness with which he spoke. It very well may have been their impact on my style and composure that made the difference in my being invited back to the Masters; there's no way to know.

The same year I broadcast at the Masters, I also was invited—actually, assigned—to announce for tennis. I worked with John Newcombe and Tony Trabert for the men's finals at the U.S. Open and with Virginia Wade and Billie Jean King for the women's finals. Billie Jean King was a famous former tennis player, but our director, Frank Chirkinian, did not want to hire her. He was forced to by some internal workings. Mark McCormack's company, IMG, had the negotiating rights to the U.S. Open and they represented Billie Jean, so Frank hired her for one year to work with Virginia Wade and me over his own objections. He didn't like the way she worked, didn't like the things she said, just flat out didn't like her.

When we later moved to the new U.S. Open site at Flushing Meadows, there were certain weather conditions in which the airplanes from LaGuardia Airport would have to take off over the stadium, and it was a big distraction. We couldn't hear anything when they were taking off or landing, although it was the takeoffs that were really bad. During the production meeting in which he was forced to hire Billie Jean, Chirkinian warned us that there was no need to do any commentary when the planes were taking off, because we were drowned out and nobody could hear what we were saying. Billie Jean either wasn't listening or didn't pay attention to what he said, because when we were on the air covering the women's final, an airplane took off and Billie Jean just kept on talking. Of course, her remarks were drowned out. I heard one of the men running the tournament press the "talk" key that the directors and producers have in their truck. I knew he was going to say something, but I couldn't imagine what. He let loose a slur about Billie Jean's sexuality into our earpieces and then said, "Don't you know that nobody can hear you when the planes are taking off like that?"

She was stunned that he would talk to her like that, and so was I. She couldn't talk to me because the audience would hear it, but when we had a commercial break, she turned to me and said, "Who is speaking to me like that?" and I said lightly, "That's God."

She knew who it was, though, from his voice, and the next time a plane took off, she continued to talk, and this time he said, "You know, Billie, when I think about it, maybe this is a break for our viewers because nobody can hear what the hell you're saying." Well, she took off her headset and quit in the middle of the broadcast, which was what I think he was trying to force her to do anyway.

I got along very well with my co-broadcasters for men's tennis, as well, and we had our fair share of interesting moments. When Newcombe was working with Trabert and me for the final, he didn't show up for rehearsal. He had a notorious reputation as a playboy womanizer. He showed up finally, just two minutes before we were supposed to go on the air, with a coat and tie on, but no shirt, and he smelled and looked like the wrath of God. I mean, he had clearly been out all night drinking. He came and sat down next to me, and Chirkinian said to him, "You no-good, Australian son of a bitch, where have you been? Why didn't you show up for rehearsal? If I have anything to do with it, you'll never work for CBS again," and then we had to go on the air.

After we got to a commercial break where I could talk, I said, "Newk, you don't have to take abuse like that. You can talk back," and he looked at me and said, "Patrick, I've learned over the years that when you're in deep shit, you don't wiggle." And he was on time from then on.

I remember how much I enjoyed doing tennis, particularly in the beginning, because Trabert and I did everything; we did the men's and the women's, even though it was only later that they gave the women's equal time with the men's, but what time they did give to the women's, Trabert and I covered together. It was a fun assignment. I had played tennis in high school and in the Florida Championship when I was sixteen, so I knew the sport. I got involved and got to know the players pretty well. I got to know Jimmy Connors extremely well. In fact, one evening when I was home, I got a phone call late at night from Gloria Connors, Jimmy's mother. She said to me, "I just want to thank you for being so nice to my son all these years during the U.S. Open," which I thought was very nice of her. Jimmy and I got to be pretty good friends—he was one of those people who could be nice to you if he liked you . . . or very discourteous if he didn't. He was subtler with his obscene gestures than John McEnroe, but could be just as bad. Connors would make like he was masturbating with his racket and often got into disputes with the chair umpire.

As I said, though, it was a pleasant assignment and something I looked forward to. However, it was a grueling time because we stayed on the air so long. As years passed, we got a demand for more airtime since tennis was in its heyday, so Trabert and I used to do the daily broadcast. We'd stay out there all day and then we'd stay and do the nightly highlights—they didn't have anybody different doing that—so we just got totally involved in the event, especially at Forest Hills, before they moved to the new arena. When the arena got bigger, so did the event and the amount of time we spent on the air. We did various tournaments around the country, none with the magnitude of the U.S. Open, but places such as Indianapolis and Newport Beach, and for the Davis Cup.

Tennis, as I said, was at its heyday at the time. A lot of people watched tennis on television and it got very popular, particularly with the New York corporate world. Every big business had a box and so did a lot of famous and important people. I also had a box at the time. That's where I got to know Don Hewitt, creator of *60 Minutes*, who was a big tennis buff and would arrive before the big crowd got there. He and Mike Wallace used to come all the time. Wilt Chamberlain was another big tennis fan who was always there, while Sophia Loren and Barbara Walters were frequent attendees. Alan King was a guest chef; he fixed hot dogs on the final Saturday every year. Most of the time Trabert and I were there, we were working on the air, but we did get to socialize a little bit, which was a really heady experience.

It was the beginning of the U.S. Open era; purses got much larger, stadiums got bigger, and so on. The quality of the Australian players when we first got on the air was very good: Newcombe, Ken Rosewall, Tony Roche. The first match I covered was between Connors and Rosewall. When I look back, I see that it really was a golden era. Today there aren't the epic rivalries that there were back then, such as between Connors and McEnroe, Bjorn Borg and Ivan Lendl, and Connors and Borg. There is no leading American anymore, either; Andre Agassi, I think, was the last.

In 1977, I covered the "winner take all" match between Connors and Elie Nastase in Puerto Rico. I remember it was very much like being on the eighteenth hole at Augusta. When I was on the air, Chirkinian, who also had been the one at Augusta who told me not to announce the winner in 1968, said to me while we were in the guts of the broadcast, "Don't say 'winner take all' again." At the next commercial break I asked him, "Why not say 'Winner take all'?" I'd used the phrase three or four times already. He answered, "Because it may not be true," and I got really incensed.

We'd had meetings that morning and we had heard rumors that Connors had gotten a guarantee and Nastase had gotten a guarantee. I specifically put a question to the producers who sponsored the tournament if it was indeed "winner take all," and they assured me that it was. I think anytime a broadcaster goes on the air and learns he's been telling a lie, it's difficult to deal with. As I mentioned, I had said "winner take all" three or four times in the opening comments and up until I got the call from Chirkinian.

I think somebody called the head of CBS Sports, Frank Barry, who is now with Mark McCormack's company, IMG, and he then called Chirkinian, who was directing, and said, "Don't mention that again while we're on the air." I got very upset that I hadn't been told; in fact, I confronted Bill Reardon, who was Connors's manager at the time and had put things together, after the match and accosted him physically. I grabbed him by the throat and said, "Why didn't you tell me this morning at the production meeting?"

It was one of those things that CBS would rather forget. The FCC and the House Committee on Energy and Commerce fined CBS heavily, because they had been aware of it. Connors had been guaranteed $500,000, and Nastase had been guaranteed $150,000. Everyone involved in the broadcast ended up getting fired from their jobs at CBS, except for Chirkinian and me. The *New York Times* got the story. Neil Amdur, who was a producer for the event and a good friend of mine, had been a writer at the *Times*, and I think he lost his job at CBS over it. This event was one of the few times that I had an audience with William Paley, the head bigwig and chief executive of CBS. He called me into his office because we had to go to Washingon and testify before the House committee. Paley said, "All I want you to do is tell the truth, no matter what it costs us as a network. I just want you to be truthful."

I don't know how I escaped the ax. I guess I was valuable to them at the time because I was broadcasting for football and golf along with tennis. I *do* know that, once again, the impact of playing for Lombardi and Landry gave me grace under pressure. I'm sure that I would have handled the situations with the "winner take all" match, Billie Jean, and John Newcombe much differently without their influence, although I can't say I consciously thought of them during those times. The level of maturity that I gained from the two of them touched on everything going forward in my career.

Of course, I'm best remembered—if I am remembered—for my work in football with my longtime broadcast partner John Madden. As I look back on my broadcasting career over the past thirty years, one of the great things about working with John Madden was that he was always the same. From the first time I worked with him, which was at a terrible game in Tampa, I saw that he had the ability that all analysts must have to make a comment that made sense in a very short time. The analyst has a very short period of time to talk, because the play-by-play man has to set the scene by discussing the down distance, the weather conditions, and the basics. Usually, until the ball is snapped and the play is over, the analyst doesn't make a comment, so there is very little time between the huddle and the next play for him to say what he has to say.

I quickly saw that Madden had an ability to make those comments and observations in a very concise way and still be clear. Obviously he had the knowledge of the game, having been the Raiders' head coach under Al Davis. Working for Davis, he saw how to put together an offense. He also had a good idea about offensive line play because he had been an offensive lineman and was a student of the game. He knew how an offensive coordinator should attack a defense and had the ability, which very few people have, to articulate that knowledge in a way that made sense.

But as I told you, he said to me many times that if people ever understood what we were talking about, we would have big problems. Well, the game has gotten so complicated, once you get past the basics, with things such as situation substitutions, pass blocking, the use of hands, what you can do to a receiver, and so on, that it's hard for most people to completely understand the intricacies of the game, the mental process that a player goes through, and the idea of never being able to literally give 100 percent—though you might try. Madden had an understanding of all those things and consistently delivered results.

A lot of guys I worked with when I was an analyst for football and other sporting events would ask me, "You feel okay today? How's your mood? You ready for the big one?" or things like that. I don't remember Madden ever asking me those questions, though, or vice versa. We were so sure of each other. I knew I was going to get his best effort and he was going to get my best effort, no matter what.

That's the good thing about broadcasting—it's as close to being a part of a team as you can get without getting hit. And not only is there a sense of camaraderie with the other broadcasters, it extends to the game as well. As a broadcaster, I got to meet the players and coaches, found out how they felt, and came close to capturing the emotions of playing in a game. At least that's what I did and I think John Madden did, too, which is what made him so successful. He could capture the feelings of the players and convey what they were trying to accomplish. That's the closest thing to playing that anyone can do.

Madden and I broadcast together for twenty-two years, and during that time we never had a cross word and never argued. We had discussions about players, teams, philosophies, things like that. We didn't always agree on the way coaches were talking about approaching a game, but we never argued. He had great respect for me because I had been a player and a broadcaster, and I had great respect for his knowledge of and approach to the game, so we sort of deferred to each other without agreeing with everything the other said.

I remember for Super Bowl XVI, we were both at CBS. It was the first indoor Super Bowl, in a domed stadium in Detroit. Everybody was a little on edge anticipating the Super Bowl, because we had been there a week, Detroit had a tremendous amount of snow, and we all were trying to get from place to place. We rehearsed over and over again the way we would bring the program on the air. After I set the scene and said what the occasion was, they would cut to us on camera and I would ask Madden two questions and, during the second question, they would go to a single shot of him while I turned around to face the field, put on my headset, and got ready for the broadcast of the game.

We had rehearsed and rehearsed and rehearsed, and Madden had answered the questions to my satisfaction, as well as the producers' and directors'. We worked on it until we were comfortable with what we had, and then went live on the air. I asked him my two questions and he was in the process of answering the second when I turned around to get ready for the coin toss and the beginning of the game. I remember the great Detroit quarterback Bobby Layne was tossing the coin. I started to put on my headset, but I couldn't find it.

There's an old adage in television that if you want to find something, just follow the cables. So I followed the cables and realized that while Madden was answering question number two, he was sitting on my headset. I had no hope of getting it out from under him, because he was a big man. I was pulling and tugging fruitlessly. Luckily, the stage manager figured out what was going on. He had an extra headset in case we had a problem, which is exactly what we had, and he gave it to me to wear. I had never used that spare headset before and it didn't fit the contour of my head, but that's how I opened Super Bowl XVI.

When Madden got through and we went to commercial, he turned and said, "What the hell's going on?" and I said, "You're sitting on my headset!" I tried to put my regular headset on, but it was all bent out of shape and unusable, so I continued using the spare headset for the rest of the game.

Everybody loves Madden because of his outrageousness and big-spiritedness during a broadcast, but he is not like that at all in real life. It was almost like John Madden the Announcer was a bombastic, arm-waving character he had created. In person, he is kind of a low-key guy and a loner, even though he was in the middle of so many people throughout his life, as a player, coach, and broadcaster. He didn't do those outrageous things that people think he did. He didn't fly, as most people know. The team he was coaching used to travel in two separate DC-3s, and one day, the plane he wasn't on crashed. He had to continue to fly for coaching, but he hated every minute of it, and after he got out of coaching, he never flew again. He had a fear of flying, of the unusual, and of heights. He would even get nervous in elevators.

Once, I was out on the field before a game, which was always my role (Madden stayed in the booth). I was talking to Al Davis and he asked me where Madden was, and I responded, "He's up in the booth. Once he gets there, he doesn't come down. He doesn't move." Davis said, "He still riding the bus?" When I answered that he was, Davis said, "He's still got that act going on, doesn't he?"

Madden was very consistent and reliable, as I said, but he had very few friends and few hobbies; his world was football. In fact, he didn't really have any friends that I knew of. He had some guys he depended on, but I don't think anybody ever really considered him to be a friend, although he was as likable a human being as you could want. I was able to penetrate his shield to a degree and am probably as good a friend as he has, and he's as good a friend as I have. I think that if something unfortunate happened to me, he'd be one of the guys I'd call on and he'd be here. He may come by bus, but he'd be here.

I think our friendship, our mutual respect for each other, and our consistency, insofar as preparation, standards, and trustworthiness went, had as much to do with our success as anything. Broadcasters have to maintain a distance from players and coaches, and there is also an unwritten understanding that broadcasters won't say certain things and won't get into certain areas during the broadcast. Ray Perkins said that we were guys who could be trusted when he introduced us to Bill Parcells, as I mentioned before, but there were some coaches who didn't feel that way. Gene Stallings, for example, did not trust us at all. When he was coaching the Cardinals, he was afraid we were going to divulge everything he was doing, so he was very reticent to talk to us. But mostly, the bond between us and the guys in the game was such that they knew there were certain things we wouldn't say, and they respected us for that. They would make comments in private with us about other players on opposing teams, for instance. They were almost always complimentary when they talked about the other teams or the other players—but there were times when they might tell us that they thought they had a good strategy to use against the opposing team, and they knew we wouldn't report on it.

Our respect and consideration for the players and coaches, along with the combination of our different personalities and styles, allowed Madden and me to stand out as broadcasters. We have been epitomized as the ultimate pair of broadcasters, which, of course, is an extreme compliment, but I don't think that either of us was ever conscious of that during our careers. Our different styles and things like that didn't really register with us, although I learned to duck when I was working with him because of his constantly swinging arms. However, the fact that we both were developing such grand reputations wasn't something that Madden or I dwelled on. Lombardi wouldn't have. Landry didn't. So we didn't, either.

CHAPTER 14

The Landry Code: Faith, Family, and Football

In a recent book, a longtime NFL writer described Tom Landry as someone who "had a lot of the absent-minded professor in him." I don't really buy that description. Landry could appear to be aloof and arrogant, but I don't think he was an absent-minded professor in any way. He had so many things going on in his mind that he might have appeared to be preoccupied, but he was always pretty tuned in. He is famous for mispronouncing names a lot—that's the extent of it. There would be situations when I'd think he had his mind on something else, yet he was really focused on what was going on with us and on the field.

The amount of attention he gave was determined by the degree of importance he placed on the situation at hand. If he didn't think talking with an NFL writer was very important, he probably wouldn't give that writer the time of day. One particular author who mentioned Landry's absentness covered the NFL for about thirty years and had that feeling. I can see how someone might mistakenly get that impression if he didn't rank high in the order of importance of things according to Landry. That's why he mispronounced so many names, such as Gary Hogeboom, for instance. He called him Hoganbloom. Hogeboom came off the bench and did astonishing things, but he was never the man in Dallas. I think the assistant coaches and their contributions were very important to Landry, not so much the names of players such as Hogeboom.

I remember once I was at a clinic at the Smithsonian Institution in Washington with Landry and Don Shula. Someone, it may have been Shula, asked Landry, "What have you been doing?," and he said he'd made a trip to Europe. When he was asked where he stayed in Paris, Landry said that he stayed in a hotel that was close to the "Lood." There was almost an innocence about that more than an absent-mindedness. Obviously, a museum in Paris wasn't really high on his importance list.

I don't recall him doing that with names during his Giants years so much. In later years, people exaggerated things like such as mispronunciation of names, and began to question his play-calling and think that the game had passed him by. At least that was the perception in the NFL; it was never really the opinion in Dallas. I certainly never subscribed to it. It seemed to me, as an observer, that he had fresh ideas all the time about what would work on offense or defense and he incorporated them into his game strategy.

For instance, the Cowboys were the first back in early days to take advantage of the computer, just as Brian Billick mentioned in his book *More Than a Game*. They used computers to evaluate talent, much more so than the other teams did, who relied more on word of mouth. Now everybody uses computers, but those were Landry innovations. They were things he, Cowboys president and manager Tex Schramm, and vice president Gil Brandt cooked up together, so although Landry might not have had a fresh approach, he had fresh ideas and was always innovating.

He was also among the first football coaches to uncover basketball players, such as Pat Riley, who was drafted by the Cowboys. The Cowboys had former basketball players as members of their defensive unit and members of their offensive unit, too. Peter Gent was a basketball player and Cornell Green was a basketball player. But I don't think there was a serious possibility that Pat Riley might have played for the Cowboys. They drafted him, but I don't think he ever came to try out. The Cowboys had hopes for him as a defensive back since they had success with Cornell Green.

Landry was a defensive genius as well, though the innovations he created and installed with the Cowboys were mostly on offense: the man in motion, the shifting, and the movement before the play ever starts—those were all Landry innovations. I really think that the people who surrounded him—Tex Schramm, chiefly—got credit for these innovations. Tex has gotten a lot of credit for the changes in the rules, the flags on top of the goalposts, and the hash marks being moved toward the center of the field. Tex was very bright, very alert, and very much involved in the competition. In fact, Tex was the head of the Competition Committee for a long, long time. I think being around Landry stimulated a lot of Tex's ideas and vice versa.

The collaboration between Tex and Landry was a change for Landry, as far as I know. As I've mentioned, there was not a lot of interplay between Lombardi and Landry on the Giants. The defense was over here and the offense was over there, and that was the way it was. Actually, there's a famous story that during one game at Yankee Stadium—I don't remember which game it was—as the offensive unit came on the field and the defensive unit came off, one of the members of the defense said to the offense, "You guys hold 'em."

The NFL writer I referenced before also mentioned that everybody in Dallas hated Jerry Jones for what he did and how he did it: cutting Landry loose. At the same time, he said, people were relieved, because he had to get out of there and there was no other way. They say—and I've heard this several times, from reliable sources—that Bum Bright, who had bought the Cowboys, had decided and told Schramm he had to get rid of Landry. It was his belief, and the belief among many people, that the game had passed Landry by and that one way or another he had to get out of it, even though he was still innovating. Yet, in the early years, when the Cowboys were an expansion team and not winning, the owner, Clint Murchison Jr., awarded Landry a ten-year contract, even when they were not winning yet. That was an extraordinary statement of faith, and Landry felt deeply indebted to him for that. Owners in later years, however, did not have the same faith in him.

During his coaching career with the Cowboys, he was very active with the Fellowship of Christian Athletes (FCA). I have no idea how much money he raised or how many speaking engagements he attended. Interestingly, when he died, they asked me if I would take his place on the board of directors, but I turned it down. There were people who thought that involvement detracted from Landry's career, that he put the FCA at number-one priority. They thought he was spending too much time with that and not enough time on football. He was going all over the country, speaking on behalf of the fellowship, and he did always put his faith first.

Maybe he did start to get set in his ways ("You do it this way or we'll get somebody else"), and, as I mentioned before, I think a lot of people got the impression that he was preoccupied with other things. "Faith, family, and football," as he said. That's the code he lived by—but only in that order. He's the only guy I've ever met who didn't compromise those standards for anything. No matter what happened, no matter what the situation, that's the way he lived his life. He was home at night for dinner with his family; he might have watched some tape in his den, but that was it. He was not the kind of coach like Joe Gibbs, who committed so much to the game that he slept at the office. A lot of that happens in football. It's almost like a fad. When John Madden and I reminisced about his coaching days, one of the things he remembered was that there was a lot of pressure on coaches to work themselves to the bone. After Dick Vermeil lost to Joe Gibbs, he started sleeping at the office, too; somehow it's easy for coaches to fall into the trap of believing that they're getting outplayed because they're being outworked. Landry wouldn't abide by that. When he wasn't at practice or at church, he was with his family.

It's not surprising that Landry got criticized for not working himself to the bone, when so many coaches felt pressured to do just that. Nobody ever really faced him down and said, "Don't you think you're spending too much time on the Fellowship of Christian Athletes?," but that was a rumbling underneath the surface. When he didn't do what other coaches were doing, people started to doubt him, I guess, and the media certainly chimed in.

The schedule during football season is so compressed that there are no days off as a head coach. Nevertheless, he'd take some time if he had an obligation to make an appearance for the FCA. He traveled to other cities to speak on days off and things like that. He had a coaching staff he could trust, and he turned the responsibility over to them. As head coach, he was responsible for the overall strategy and plan, but he could let his coordinators deal with the nitty-gritty and get tactical while he took time off. If it were a local appearance, he would take half a day off or nights. He was involved in every aspect of the game, no mistake about that, but he would delegate responsibility, much like Jim Lee Howell did, to either Ermal Allen or one of his other very capable assistants. I think, in his case, the assistants had a lot of authority. However, even though he did that, the concept of head coach as absolute dictator was something he bought into, and he wondered why other coaches didn't. Bud Grant was like that; he'd call practice at the end of the day and go hunting on Fridays. Vikings' practice wouldn't take place until he was done hunting. Grant was oblivious to the pressure of what other people did. He did it his way and didn't worry about it, and so did Landry.

I think that by doing what he did, Landry was teaching two huge lessons: the value of balance and perspective, and the courage to follow your beliefs. Just because you have job security doesn't mean you're going to pursue balance. The way work invades every moment afflicts all of society, especially because of technology like the Internet and cell phones. I don't think Landry would be carrying around a BlackBerry if he were coaching today or that he would let the game infiltrate every aspect of his life. He had the ability, like most great athletes, to block everything else out when he needed to and center on the task at hand. As players, Johnny Unitas had that ability, and I think Peyton Manning seems to have that ability today. If you watch Drew Brees, he has that ability as well.

I remember experiencing that a couple of times myself. I would go out on the field during a crucial situation and there would be seventy-five thousand people there, yet I was totally oblivious to them and what was going on around me. When I centered in like that, I wasn't conscious of anything except the task at hand, and I think Landry was able to tap into that extreme focus, to block everything else out and become involved in his own little capsule—and that extended to how he organized his schedule for speaking engagements during the season.

I don't know if that ability is something that can be learned. I wish I did know for sure, but my feeling is that some people are born with it. I think Jack Nicklaus, in particular, was oblivious to his surroundings when he was concentrating. The media try to make something out of pressure, such as in a World Series, a Super Bowl, or another championship game. However, if a player has that focus, he doesn't feel that pressure and he doesn't consider the surroundings or think about the consequences if he makes or misses. That ability is something you can't teach, and I don't think I've ever heard a coach discuss how to do it. I think most players aren't able to block out everything else at the necessary moment. Having that ability is one of the things about greatness that rarely gets mentioned.

Landry was not only able to close out the surroundings of the field as a player, but also the critics when he was coaching. I think he did it in life, too, with his devotion to his standards. He never lowered them or made adjustments because of convenience or because of media opinion on what he ought to do. It's not that the game passed him by; it's that he continued to insist on standards in an era when standards went out of style.

I remember talking with Ken Venturi, who worked with me for a long time on golf broadcasts and who had a bad stutter. He'd talk about how much golf helped him conquer his stuttering. His devotion helped him block everything else out and he could control what he was doing, which allowed him to overcome it. We have a preacher in a church in Dallas who also stutters. Can you imagine choosing a profession of preaching if you stutter? He was a quarterback at Baylor and often said to me, as well as in his sermons, "You've noticed by now that I stutter. But it only bothers me if I talk." His mantra is, "If I can do it, y-y-y-you can." Landry, as I said, could shut out distractions both on the field and off; because of that same devotion and because of that talent, he was able to live his life by his standards. If that meant going on a speaking trip for the FCA, so be it.

His ability influenced my ability in broadcasting to focus in and listen to two people talking to me in different ears at the same time, along with the analyst. I remember not too long ago, at last year's Super Bowl, the former Buccaneers free and strong safety John Lynch was just beginning his broadcasting career and he asked me for advice. I told him to just have the ability to listen, to block out the outside influences, and to listen to what you want to listen to and he said, "Nobody's ever told me that before."

In terms of preparation and being ready to do what has to be done, observing Lombardi and Landry's methods probably made me stay up later at night preparing for a broadcast—another big lesson. In my professional career, I had never been exposed to that kind of attention to detail. Witnessing that certainly had a strong effect on me, which lasted throughout my days as a broadcaster. One of the first things broadcaster Chris Schenkel told me was, "If you think you're going to have five minutes on the air, prepare a half hour." And I could follow that advice because I'd seen from Lombardi and Landry what it takes to be prepared.

And usually, my preparation paid off—but, of course, you can't anticipate everything. I was once covering a game in the Cotton Bowl before the Cowboys moved to Texas Stadium. I was the analyst for the game, and the producers in New York had decided it would be a good idea to send the analyst down to the field to introduce both teams. So I went down to the sideline to introduce the players and staff, and I got through the entire defensive unit of the St. Louis Cardinals. Then I went through the Cowboys' offensive unit without a glitch, getting everyone's name correct. And then suddenly I got to Tom Landry, and I drew a blank. I had played for him; I had broadcast his games; I had admired him . . . and I couldn't remember his name. Something in his face changed, and I could see that he sensed I'd drawn a blank.

He said, "I'm the coach of the Dallas Cowboys. My name is Tom Landry."

"Thank you, Coach," I answered. And the broadcast went on.

Nerves are the biggest culprit for interfering with preparation. I would get cases of nerves, not so much during football broadcasts, since I had enough knowledge in the bank to fill the time, but in golf, I can remember thinking, "What am I going to say? How am I going to put this?" I would mull over things—not liking the way things came out or not liking what I said, especially when my knowledge of the subject was not what it should have been. I think as I became comfortable in my knowledge of the subject and gained confidence in my ability, I became less nervous.

Nowadays, though, I hear broadcasters spouting statistics and I sit there as a fan and think, "Did he study that or did someone just whisper that in his ear?" A lot of today's broadcasters prepare so much that they get on the air and feel obligated to use what they've prepared, whether it applies or not. Learning to listen and to apply capsule judgments helped me stay away from that pitfall.

I also didn't have to compete for time with three people in the booth, two more on the sidelines, five before the game, and three at halftime. It's like all those assistant coaches; everybody's trying to make their mark instead of create a great broadcast. You can definitely draw a parallel between all those assistant coaches and all the guys in the announcing booth, and the analogy extends to the resulting mediocrity today of both play and broadcasting. Those broadcasters don't have the rhythm that Madden and I had. It's every man for himself, and the fear is, "If I don't make a mark, if I don't say something, I'm going to get graded down." They know that the executives back in L.A. or New York are listening and evaluating them based on their preparation and the nuggets they come up with, whatever they may be.

To compensate, people overprepare. I sometimes felt underprepared going into a game. I always tried to have as much knowledge as I could, but I drew a line. I worked with one particular individual who had prepped with what kind of pajamas the player wore, and listening to that in rehearsal, I thought, "Who cares?" I think I was always prepared with enough pertinent information, information I thought was important.

Judgment has a lot to do with making that call. I know that all Hank Stram, a former head coach, looked at was the turnover, with the thinking that if you led the league in turnovers, you would more often than not be in the Super Bowl, and he was usually right. Only looking at that statistic was his philosophy, and I heard somebody say that no matter what the era was, if you listened to Hank Stram's broadcast, it would apply, which is probably true. But each team takes on its own complexion, and it's up to the broadcaster to find out what that team has confidence in and what they don't have confidence in, what they believe they can do and what they don't believe they can do. It's up to the broadcaster to find out what, in his opinion, the team excels at and what it doesn't; that's what the fans expect us to know.

I don't think Schenkel's advice about research and preparation would have meant as much if I hadn't had those experiences with Lombardi and Landry. They gave me a context for seeing what preparation meant. The lesson I took from Landry was that we all need intense preparation, but not at the cost of creating imbalance in our lives; and that we must block out all distractions, whether they be disturbances when we're focusing on our work or people criticizing us for living by our values. A man astute enough to know and live by those lessons could not have been passed by, by the game or by life. Until the end, he was always just as focused as he was back in 1958 on what really mattered to him.

At the end of the next season, Landry got a job with the Cowboys. We had heard rumors that it was going to happen, of course, but we had thought that if Lombardi didn't get the head coaching job that it would have been Landry.

I had had more one-on-one time with him than most or perhaps any of the other players because he was my kicking coach. When he decided to leave New York, he called me into his apartment on the Grand Concourse in the Bronx. He told me, "I'm going to be the coach of the Cowboys. You might beat me someday, but whether you do or not, there's a few things I want you to remember." Then he gave me playing advice, just as if we were in a regular practice and not parting ways.

Landry told me I didn't have to worry about distance with my kicks, but what I had to work on was direction. He explained what I was most likely doing wrong if I missed a kick to the right, and what was wrong if I missed to the left. And then he said, "Don't ever practice kicking without somebody supervising who knows what's right and what's wrong. If you practice unsupervised, you'll develop bad habits. It doesn't do anybody any good to practice bad habits."

I carried his advice with me throughout my football career. I never kicked without a discerning, outside eye watching me from the sidelines. But it wasn't until many years later that I realized that when Landry told me it wouldn't do me any good to practice bad habits, he was talking about more than just kicking. I'd like to imagine that after all that time, it was his way of showing he cared about the direction I took in life. It was his way of expressing warmth.

That Landry would do something like that, even though it might cost him a win in the future, made me think about what a good, kindhearted man he was. I thought, "He really is concerned about me, not just what's going on with this team." For the first time, I had the sense that he really cared about me—even through I'd gone through years without knowing the man even had feelings. He did. It just wasn't his way to communicate them. But that's how I knew he did care.

CHAPTER 15

The Lombardi Code: Speak Confidently and Prepare

ff the football field, Lombardi taught me two other things that defined my life going forward: the importance of speaking confidently and, just like Landry, the value of preparation. As I've said, his certainty in his ways was what I admire most about him, and I knew he couldn't achieve it without confidence and preparation. He taught me how to be ready in any different situation: if anybody asked a question or had doubts about a play, he was always ready to disprove any fears.

I don't think I ever had another model like Lombardi when it came to expressing myself clearly and succinctly. I worked early on in broadcasting with Ray Scott. He was a legend in Green Bay and did the Packers' games there. He expressed himself with an economy of words and didn't use lot of flowery phrases, but he had such a voice that what he said made anyone sit up and listen. Early in my career, I watched how he did things and realized that I didn't need to speak a lot to say a lot; television is a visual medium, and the picture tells most of the story. Broadcasters don't have to magnify or glorify for people what they can already see.

Lombardi knew that. The way he explained the in-sweep, for example, or the trap play—something as insignificant as that—was mesmerizing. It was almost like someone reading to you from a great novel because of the dramatic way Coach Lombardi would set the scene for the play. In a trap play, you trick one of the defensive players to cross the line of scrimmage, thus creating a hole your running back can run through. Lombardi's gift was to know, and to describe, every single essential detail in the course of defending against a trap play (or any play, for that matter). In the case of a trap, he would show how defensive linemen were to react to a trap. Who would be making the most important block: the center on the off-tackle. How many steps the back would take. Exactly how long his steps should be. "This man has to pivot with his left foot first, to avoid getting entangled with his quarterback. Your guard has to take this step first, then that step next." And so on.

Those intricate things wouldn't interest other people, but we football players were breathless with excitement and anticipation as Coach Lombardi took us through the play. He would spend an entire half hour just on defending the trap. He would be emotional as he explained what made his approach work. We were all sitting on the edges of our chairs, even though we had been running this play since junior high school . . . and even though we had heard him take us through the same play many times before. He would build to a crescendo as he demonstrated each player's responsibility. Was it like listening to a religious sermon? Believe me, it was. We knew it was special, because we had never seen a coach so detail-oriented; so passionate; and above all, so correct. That's why we all loved Lombardi, even though he treated us all the same way. Like dogs!

He had such a knowledge and deep command of his material and presented all the nuances and details of every play in such a fashion that there was no way I could forget anything he said. He was that great a teacher. When I watched Lombardi, I don't know that I was consciously deciding to emulate him, but I do remember thinking, "If I could only be that way . . . if I could only say things as confidently as he says them."

I never thought I accomplished that, though. I don't think any broadcasters ever reach complete satisfaction in their work, but

I did succeed in learning a couple of key things about doing the job as best I could. Once, we were doing a game in Tampa against the Giants. Lombardi's wife, Marie, was feared and respected just as much as he was, and she also remained a very close friend of the Mara family, so they were in the booth next to us. I was rehearsing before the game and Tom Brookshier, with whom I was working at the time, was late. For once, the two of us had gone to bed the night before the game and gotten a good night's sleep, so I assumed that if he wasn't in the booth yet, he was in the production truck.

This is how I got a good lesson about the dangers of the microphone: I didn't realize we were feeding our rehearsal to all of the luxury boxes in the Tampa stadium, and I said, "Hey, Tom, you in the truck?" He was, so I said, "Hey, Tom, we made a big mistake last night. They tell me if we had gone out with the rest of the guys, the pickings were so good that Quasimodo, the Hunchback of Notre Dame, could have gotten laid in the joint we were supposed to go to."

Soon after, the back door of the booth popped open, and it was Marie Lombardi. "I heard what you just said on the air. You've got to be more careful with what you say on the microphone. You're one of my Vinny's boys."

I said to her, by way of an apology, "I'm sorry, but I didn't think we were feeding into the stadium. I thought the microphone was dead."

"No," she answered. "I heard what you said."

The Mara family always had a priest in their box, so I asked her, "Would you please apologize to Father Dudley? I'm sorry you heard what I said. I certainly didn't mean for you to hear it. I'll have to be more careful."

She started to walk away and then she turned to me and said, with a grin, "Well, *did* you?"

That's something that I never forgot again: any time a mike is in front of me, it might be live. I guess the consequence of how I presented myself through my words was the ultimate lesson I learned from both Lombardi *and* his wife.

I got the opportunity to put my lessons from Lombardi to work through a random opportunity. When I was still playing for the Giants, we were staying in a hotel during a game, and Charlie Conerly was my roommate. The phone rang and it was for Conerly, but he was in the shower and couldn't answer. I didn't know who was on the line, but I told him that Charlie couldn't come to the phone, but I'd be glad to give him a message, and he said, "Just remind him that he has to be at CBS today at four o'clock this afternoon to read an audition script."

I said I would certainly remind him that he had an appointment.

I was just about an inch from hanging up the receiver when I heard the caller say something. I couldn't make out what it was, so I put the receiver back to my ear and said, "I'm sorry?"

He repeated, "Well, what are *you* doing this afternoon?"

I said, "I'm either going to go somewhere and drink beer with the boys or go to a movie or something. I have no plans."

So the fellow said, "Why don't you come along and read the same script?"

There were four of us who read: Alex Webster, Kyle Rote, Conerly, and me. The job was a five-minute network radio show being written by a guy named Dave Camerer. They were looking for an active player, and it was all scripted. All I had to do was read. The show was split; there were thirteen weeks devoted to football, and the other thirty-nine weeks were devoted to baseball. Yankee shortstop Phil Rizzuto covered the thirty-nine weeks of baseball, and whoever they chose out of the football program would do the other thirteen weeks. They ended up picking me out of the bunch.

The program was mostly taped, but sometimes it was live. That experience was what made me realize that I wanted to be in broadcasting. I was making more from doing that radio spot than I was playing for the Giants. The idea that I could get paid good money and not get hit was sort of a revelation.

I'm not sure why they picked me over the other three. I always had that ability to read well, I guess, and God blessed me with a voice that they accepted. Certainly, listening to the way Lombardi spoke with confidence and authority had a big effect on me, especially when I was first doing the show. I had to learn what it takes to build that confidence, and I concluded that it was preparation. My work ethic definitely became a lot more dedicated from listening to him. I recognized the enormous amount of preparation that was needed to back his level of assurance.

He was the complete opposite of the hemming and hawing Cardinals coaches. Lombardi could answer any question, and if you had a question about what would happen in a certain situation during a play that he put up—because inevitably, in football, the unexpected will happen—his catchall phrase was: "Then you react like a football player." If you had the ultimate challenge or something he couldn't answer specifically, that's what he'd fall back on. Later, there were particular situations when I would tell myself to react like a broadcaster. Once, a player didn't show up for a live interview, and the director said to me, "We've got eighteen minutes of empty airtime, and you're going to cover it. Think of everything you know about football and say it." I still don't remember anything I said then, but I suppose I did all right. I reacted like a broadcaster.

Anyway, those five-minute segments reading in the studio got me comfortable in front of the microphone. I think that experience made me more cognizant and appreciative of the importance of pronunciation and the basics of public speaking. I also came to see the significance of preparation in the broadcasting context, because Dave Camerer, who had been a football player at Dartmouth College, and I would talk at various times during the week while he was preparing, and he would write based on my thoughts and incorporate some of his thoughts as well.

After that job, I retired from football and was hired as the analyst for the Giants' games. I worked with Chris Schenkel, who also had a great preparation ethic. By this time, Lombardi, Landry, and Howell were gone, and Allie Sherman was head coach. It was strange to come back to the Giants as a broadcaster and not have those three around, although I had played for Sherman for a year in 1961 and already knew it wasn't the same. Sherman had traded Sam Huff to Washington and Rosey Grier to the Rams. I think he was trying to break up the Landry nucleus because he wanted his own guys in there. Dick Modzelewski had already retired, and he and Grier had been key parts of that defense. Harland Svare, Cliff Livingston, and Jimmy Patton had retired, too. I retired because I had been exposed to the broadcasting business and was making more money doing that. I had kids by then and was ready to settle down. Moving them and my wife to New York, living in the Concourse Plaza Hotel for two or three years, and then living in Scarsdale, north of New York City, was like having a nomad's life. I was only thirty-one and as a kicker I could have played a lot more, maybe another ten or fifteen years, but I was ready for a change.

Allie Sherman had gotten the job Lombardi should have gotten, broken up the team that was my team, traded my friends, and tried to break up the Landry influence, so I didn't have the warmest feelings in the world toward him when I was broadcasting the Giants' games. Neither did the fans, who had "Good-bye, Allie" signs and songs.

He had a totally different offensive philosophy from Lombardi. Lombardi took the "kill the chief and the rest of the people will quit" approach. His mentality was that we should defeat their best player and the rest of them would lower their resistance as a result. Sherman believed that you should find the weak spot and attack that weak spot.

I liked Lombardi's view better; it simply worked better. As I look back on it, the fact that we had superior, intelligent personnel back then probably helped things work better, but at the time, I attributed our success to Lombardi's philosophy. It was a very gutsy, manly approach, and it seemed to work because our strengths were such that we could usually go after their best player effectively. I think in the so-called Greatest Game Ever Played, the Colts realized that we couldn't cover Raymond Berry, that our personnel were inferior to their personnel, and so he caught twelve passes.

Sherman didn't have an outstanding record with the Giants. His breaking up the team was the biggest thing that really rubbed me the wrong way. He thought he was a better offensive teacher than Lombardi and thought his method was better than Lombardi's. I didn't buy into that. Of course, Lombardi was not the legend then that he is today. He didn't have the reputation yet, but the quality was there. I suppose Sherman thought that his method of attack would be more effective in the long run. It seems to me that was something he talked himself into, though, since he ultimately didn't have the success Lombardi did.

As serious as Lombardi was about football, though, he also knew what it meant to be loyal to players and to have respect for their personal lives—which is something Sherman didn't seem to have when he made those trades. I can even remember instances when players' lives were even *more* important to Lombardi than practice time. The moment that stands out to me the most was in that season of '58. I walked into the locker room one day, and Lombardi met me just inside the door.

He said, "Go home."

"What for?" I asked.

It would be unheard of that practice was canceled. I couldn't imagine what was going on.

"Your daughter fell and knocked out one of her front teeth. Go home; you're needed at home."

And I went.

That was typical of the way both Lombardi and Landry handled family situations. Today, if a player went to his coach and said, "My daughter lost a tooth. Can I skip practice this afternoon?," I'm sure the answer would be "no" in no uncertain terms. And if the coach got the news before the player, he'd probably keep it to himself until after practice. But to Lombardi, a hurt daughter—whether she had a broken tooth or a broken arm—was an emergency, and I went home.

As a broadcaster, I had to stay consistent and put my nostalgia for Landry and Lombardi and my personal feelings for Sherman in my back pocket so I could cover the game. I'm sure I wasn't very good at it in the beginning. In fact, I know I wasn't. We did a game every week, because we followed the team, and as I mentioned before, during the broadcast I referred to the Giants as "we." I got back to New York after broadcasting a couple of games, and the brass at CBS told me, "Don't refer to your team as 'we.'" I was supposed to be someone who was at least neutral, even though I was only doing the Giants' games.

The broadcasting process was a little bit different in those years, because back then we had two sets of announcers for every game. Philadelphia had its own set of announcers, Pittsburgh had its own set of announcers, the Giants had their own set of announcers, and so on. The broadcast would go from the Philadelphia announcers, via their production truck, to the Philadelphia audience and from the Pittsburgh announcers to the Pittsburgh audience. The New York audience, which at that time stretched up into New England, just got me and Schenkel. Then, in about 1964 or 1965, they started to use only one set of announcers, so the audiences in Philadelphia, Pittsburgh, and everywhere else got me and Schenkel instead of their own announcers. I think the television network did that to reduce the "homers" influence and to reduce their costs as well.

They told me to be impartial and not to just call it from a Giants viewpoint, but that was hard to do, because we only covered the Giants. We did the Giants every week and got very familiar with them. I don't think the Giants' fans objected to me calling the Giants "we." They probably felt themselves included in that collective "we." People were very passionate about the Giants. I remember when people would drive to other cities or areas to see the Giants broadcast. The blackout rule was in force most of the time, so the games could be blacked out locally. If you wanted to see the Giants broadcast, you had to be outside the seventy-five-mile radius from Yankee Stadium. Some bars within the radius had Giants games, which is what I think ultimately led to them lifting the blackout rule. I don't know how they did it, but these bars stole the signal somehow and would have signs that said, "We get the Giants games." The way the blackout rule was supposed to work was that any home game that wasn't sold out couldn't be broadcast locally.

I hope my opinions of Sherman didn't color the broadcast, but I'm sure they did. I remember sitting in the booth, thinking, "What did he do that for?" We weren't permitted to question a lot of what the coaches or players were doing, though. We basically had to go on what we saw and heard from various players and sources we talked to. The expression for what we were required to do was "calling the ball"—meaning that we stuck to what we saw on the field. A very limited amount of my own personality was allowed to go into the broadcast; it was all about calling the ball.

People are surprised sometimes at just how little talking old baseball or football broadcasters did, but we didn't have a lot of the mechanical things they have now: no writing on the screen, no instant replay, no Elias Sports Bureau—although it probably existed, we just didn't utilize it. There was just very little information. We had the passing statistics that we kept next to us, but that was about it. We had a spotter and a statistician, but Schenkel used the same spotter, I think, for everything.

In the beginning, there were three people I primarily worked with as an analyst: Chris Schenkel, Jack Buck, and Ray Scott, and I think I learned from each of them. When I started to do play-by-play, I was confident enough in my ability to do it; however, that was after I had been doing the analyst job for about ten years. I started to do play-by-play in 1971. Bill MacPhail, who had been the head of CBS Sports, was a close friend of mine, but he thought I was an analyst and that was it.

Bob Wussler took MacPhail's place, and one day he called me at my home in New Jersey, where I was living at the time. "I need to talk to you. Can you come into the office?"

Naturally, I picked up and went to the office as fast as I could. When I got there, he said, "I have to break you two people up."

I was working with Jack Buck at the time, who I liked very much. Wussler said, "You and Jack sound just alike. I can't tell who's talking."

So I said to him, on the spur of the moment, "Well, as long as you're going to break us up, I think I'd like to try to do play-by-play."

He asked me who I wanted to work with, but I couldn't come up with a name off the top of my head. He told me to think about it, and then I asked him when he wanted me to start. This was in the middle of the season, and I thought he would say, "Let's get some games on tape and see how you sound and if you're ready to do it . . ." and so on, but he said, "Next week." This was on a Tuesday and I thought, "My gosh, I don't know if I'm ready to do that."

Finally, I named Tom Brookshier as the person I wanted to work with, because Brookie and I had been working at the NFL film headquarters on a weekly show. I knew we were compatible, as much as I hated him when we played against each other, and I knew we could get along on the air. Wussler contacted Brookshier and told him what he was doing, and so we did the Cardinals versus Giants game in the middle of the season in St. Louis. I did the play-by-play and he did the color. The only thing I remember about our first broadcast together is that we went for breakfast Sunday morning before the game and he said, "The play-by-play man always buys breakfast."

He is probably as close to anybody as I've ever gotten and most like a brother of anybody I've ever known. Later, he was the one who cared about me enough to be the front man for my intervention. It was ironic because Brookshier was a wild man when whiskey was involved. I think that's one of the reasons they broke us up: they were afraid that somebody was going to end up dead—we certainly enjoyed life. We enjoyed broadcasting together, too. We made a great team.

I would think about Lombardi and the effectiveness and authority with which he spoke many times when I was broadcasting. When I was sure of something, he popped into my mind. I don't think I can overemphasize the effect he had on my style of speaking. He made me understand that if I were sure about what I was talking about, it would come through and people would read that certainty.

I'm known for an economy of words in my broadcasts; Lombardi also was thrifty with his words. I modeled my "get to the point, say what you need to say, and don't say anything else" style on what he taught. The only time anyone ever commanded my attention the way he did was when I was at the Betty Ford Center, being treated for alcoholism. Dr. James West, who was one of the founders, came in to teach a class, and I thought, "My gosh, he's like Lombardi," because he knew what he was talking about so thoroughly, and when he spoke, he commanded my attention. It was like my first day of Giants training camp, when Lombardi came in and cleared his throat and a hush fell over the room.

In the years when he was coaching the Packers and the Redskins and when I was broadcasting, I think he got to be more aware as a coach. He ran everything in Green Bay; he was the general manager and the coach all rolled into one. Everybody at CBS was deathly afraid of him, so if anybody had a request for him anytime we did a Packers game, they would lean on me to ask, because of our friendship. He refused me very few times, and although there might have been times when he didn't want to do what they requested, he would do it for me. Other than that, though, I don't think he really changed. Our relationship didn't change; it always felt like he was a friend. The position and fame he achieved didn't change the way he treated me, and I still called him Vinny. All the players on the Giants called him that. The backup players spoke with reverence and called him "Coach," but the regular Giants players, I guess since he was an assistant, called him Vinny and continued to.

When Lombardi passed away, I don't remember where I was, but I do remember talking to people who knew about it and asking, "What caused him to die?" Somebody said he had cancer, and I remember the response was, "Cancer wouldn't dare."

If I could say something to Vince Lombardi now, I would tell him my appreciation for the lessons he taught me. I would say, "Thank you very much. You had a great influence on my life. Because of you, I learned the value of preparation and of knowing how to speak with confidence.

"But most of all, I think that because of you, I learned how to be a better man."

Landry and Lombardi did make me into a Giant. But they also made me a better human being, a better teacher, a better communicator, and better at coming to terms with faith and with my own responsibilities as a man. Those gifts have stayed with me . . . for more than fifty years.

INDEX